THE ARUNDELLS OF WARDOUR

TO

MY GRANDCHILDREN: JAKE, TOBY, OSCAR,

JULIETTE AND ANNIE

in the hope that they will one day enjoy exploring Wardour

THE ARUNDELLS
OF WARDOUR

From Cornwall to Colditz

BARRY WILLIAMSON

First published in the United Kingdom in 2011
by The Hobnob Press, PO Box 1838, East Knoyle, Salisbury, SP3 6FA
www.hobnobpress.co.uk

British Library Cataloguing in Publication Data
A catalogue record for this book is available from the British Library

ISBN 978-1-906978-12-9

Typeset in Scala 11/16 pt. Typesetting and origination by John Chandler
Printed by Lightning Source

Contents

John, 16th and last Lord Arundell with his sister Isabel at the east door of Wardour Castle on 8 January 1929.

Prologue

ON 26 March 1940, John Arundell, 16th Lord Arundell of Wardour arrived late at night at Tisbury station in Wiltshire. He walked home in the brilliant moonlight, past Wallmead Farm and Beethoven Cottage to the great mansion which his ancestor had built in the 18th century. The house was locked but John knew a secret entrance behind the high altar in the chapel. He made his way silently through the room where his mother was sleeping to his own bedroom on an upper floor.

During the next few days John visited all the tenants on the Wardour estate to say goodbye before he returned to France where he was serving with the Wiltshire Regiment. He walked to Ansty, past the ruins of the old castle and under the dry stone arch. The whole village belonged to him and it took a long time to visit everyone. He sat in the Parsons' kitchen talking about his plans to improve the village once the war was over; he intended to provide piped water to all the cottages and modern drainage throughout the village. Les Parsons remembered his modesty and kind interest in everyone. Mrs Morgan in Wardour was cleaning shoes when he called at St Mary's cottage. Patrick Fagan, his nephew, was in the nursery in the castle with his sister Deidre when John came to say goodbye.

Just over four years later, there was jubilation at Wardour Castle and on the estate. Lady Arundell received a telegram on 14 September 1944 saying that John would be returning home during the following week. He was being repatriated owing to ill health after more than four years in German prison camps, latterly at Colditz. Preparations were made rapidly; an arch with Welcome Home was put over the castle gate, bonfires were prepared . . . Then came another telegram saying that John had disembarked at Liverpool but was critically ill in hospital at Chester, suffering from TB. Lady Arundell and her daughters Blanche and Isabel, travelled through the night to his bedside. He knew them and was able to say goodbye. He died in the early hours of 25 September, the 16th and last Lord Arundell. With his death the title became extinct and the castle and estate were inherited by a distant cousin who changed his name to Arundell as a condition of his inheritance.

In a sense, that is the end of the story which stretches back over nearly 500 years and begins with a group of schoolboys in Oxford at the end of the 15th century and their teacher, Thomas Wolsey. In those intervening years, the Arundells lived close to King Henry VIII, served and endured the anger of Queen Elizabeth I, saw their castle blown up in the Civil War, arranged a series of 'good' marriages, built the largest Georgian mansion in Wiltshire, supported the adventures of Sir Richard Burton, and, in the person of John, joined the fight against the evils of Nazi tyranny. Running through all those years was an unwavering devotion to the Catholic faith and for that the family suffered nearly 250 years of fines, prohibitions, exclusions, and persecution. The Arundell estates came to the family originally as a reward for service at the court of Henry VIII. They reached their greatest extent in the late 18th century when they were located in seven different counties and covered over 40,000 acres. The Arundells were undoubtedly 'great landowners' but the 8th Lord, at the very end of the 18th century, suffered one of the largest bankruptcies of any individual in that century of profligate spenders. Thereafter, the estates were reduced to the size that would sustain only an average Wiltshire squire, not a lord with five houses and a prominent place in Society.

My interest in Wardour began as a boy in the 1940s and 1950s when I lived in Swallowcliffe on the edge of the estate. My mother was the village schoolteacher and a great exponent of 'learning outside the classroom'. She was always keen to take children out of school on nature walks which were interpreted liberally. She closed the school in June 1948 and again in September 1952 to take everyone to the sales of the contents of the new castle. She said we were seeing history made. On sunny days, which were very frequent then, there were school visits to the ruins of the old castle where we were admitted free because, 'Lord Arundell said that anyone living on the estate did not need to pay, ever.' My mother told us the story of the castle during the Civil War, of how Lady Arundell had thrown her jewels down a well before she was taken as a prisoner to Shaftesbury (when could we start digging?) and of how a white owl flew from the towers of the castle whenever the Arundells were about to suffer tragedy and misfortune (the last time it was seen was in September 1944). She said that the family had to sell Wardour Street in London to pay for the new castle and it seemed extraordinary to us that anyone could own a whole street. And someone called Isabel had made a great bonfire near the castle and burned all her husband's books and papers . . . myths and legends in plenty.

The new castle at Wardour, built by the 8th Lord in the 1770s with the old castle in the background, drawn by P. Crocker in the 1820s.

This book does not aim to be a detailed study of every generation of the Arundells since the 16th century. Family history can be as boring as reading a telephone directory, especially when very little is known about the lives of some individuals. I've therefore chosen a few members of the family who are particularly significant and used the family papers now deposited in the Wiltshire & Swindon Archives to try to hear them speak. Of course the papers that would be the most useful are usually missing – letters, diaries, personal memorabilia. The 8th Lord kept a journal but only a few pages have survived. There are no letters from the 'Disastrous Dowager'. John's letters and cards from prisons in Germany have been lost. But a rich collection remains and this is the story of some of the Arundells of Wardour.

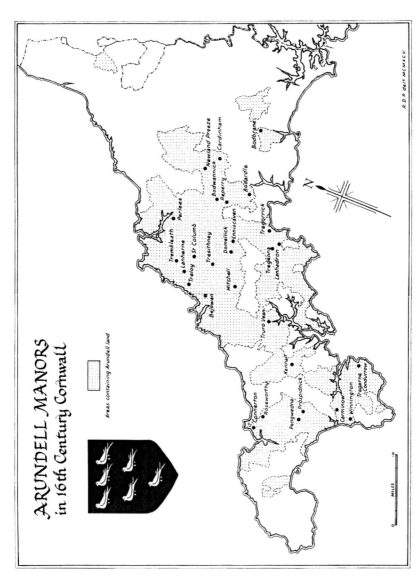

ARUNDELL MANORS
in 16th Century Cornwall

Areas containing Arundell land

The Arundells owned the largest estate in Cornwall in the 16th century. (Cornwall Record Office)

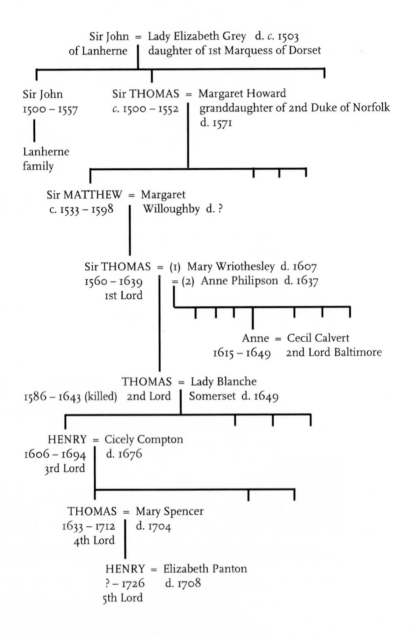

Sir John = Lady Elizabeth Grey d. *c.* 1503
of Lanherne | daughter of 1st Marquess of Dorset

Sir John
1500 – 1557

Sir THOMAS = Margaret Howard
c. 1500 – 1552 | granddaughter of 2nd Duke of Norfolk
d. 1571

Lanherne
family

Sir MATTHEW = Margaret
c. 1533 – 1598 | Willoughby d. ?

Sir THOMAS = (1) Mary Wriothesley d. 1607
1560 – 1639 | = (2) Anne Philipson d. 1637
1st Lord

Anne = Cecil Calvert
1615 – 1649 2nd Lord Baltimore

THOMAS = Lady Blanche
1586 – 1643 (killed) 2nd Lord | Somerset d. 1649

HENRY = Cicely Compton
1606 – 1694 | d. 1676
3rd Lord

THOMAS = Mary Spencer
1633 – 1712 | d. 1704
4th Lord

HENRY = Elizabeth Panton
? – 1726 d. 1708
5th Lord

The Earlier Arundells (simplified). The head of the family is in capitals.

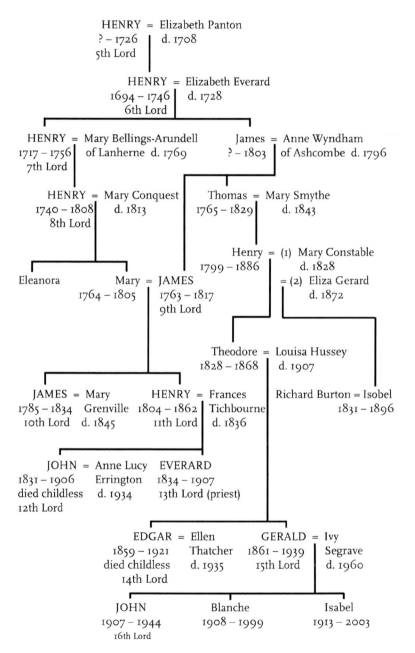

HENRY = Elizabeth Panton
? – 1726 | d. 1708
5th Lord

HENRY = Elizabeth Everard
1694 – 1746 | d. 1728
6th Lord

HENRY = Mary Bellings-Arundell   James = Anne Wyndham
1717 – 1756 | of Lanherne d. 1769   ? – 1803 | of Ashcombe d. 1796
7th Lord

HENRY = Mary Conquest   Thomas = Mary Smythe
1740 – 1808 | d. 1813   1765 – 1829 | d. 1843
8th Lord

Henry = (1) Mary Constable
1799 – 1886 | d. 1828
= (2) Eliza Gerard
d. 1872

Eleanora   Mary = JAMES
1764 – 1805 | 1763 – 1817
9th Lord

Theodore = Louisa Hussey
1828 – 1868 | d. 1907

JAMES = Mary   HENRY = Frances   Richard Burton = Isobel
1785 – 1834 | Grenville   1804 – 1862 | Tichbourne   1831 – 1896
10th Lord | d. 1845   11th Lord | d. 1836

JOHN = Anne Lucy   EVERARD
1831 – 1906 | Errington   1834 – 1907
died childless | d. 1934   13th Lord (priest)
12th Lord

EDGAR = Ellen   GERALD = Ivy
1859 – 1921 | Thatcher   1861 – 1939 | Segrave
died childless | d. 1935   15th Lord | d. 1960
14th Lord

JOHN   Blanche   Isabel
1907 – 1944   1908 – 1999   1913 – 2003
16th Lord

The Later Arundells (simplified). The head of the family is in capitals.

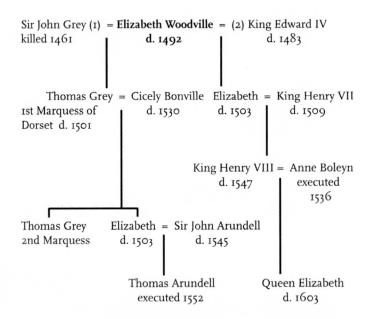

The Arundells and the Royal Family

1

Thomas the Founder

ABOUT the year 1516, a young man made his way from Cornwall to London to seek fame and fortune. Thomas Arundell, born about 1500,[1] was the younger son of Sir John Arundell of Lanherne. But this is not a rags to riches story. Thomas came from the wealthiest and most powerful family in Cornwall.[2] They owned land in 21 manors and were known as 'The Great Arundells'. Thomas was talented and energetic and must have thought that Cornwall was too small a territory for his abilities, unlike most of his family who were happy to stay there all their lives. Thomas had another great advantage – a network of useful connections with powerful people that would bring him close to the greatest in the land.

The story should perhaps begin in Oxford and not in Cornwall or London with a schoolteacher and his pupils at Magdalen College School in about the year 1498. The teacher was Thomas Wolsey,[3] 'an honest, poor man's son, born in Ipswich' and he is surely one of the most famous schoolteachers in History. On this occasion his pupils were the Grey boys, the three sons of the 1st Marquess of Dorset, son of Edward IV's queen, Elizabeth Woodville, by her first marriage. The Marquess was very pleased with Wolsey's work as his sons' teacher and invited him to spend Christmas with the family in 1499. He then rewarded him in 1500 with his first benefice, the rectory of Limington in Somerset. Wolsey was launched on the career that took him to Lord Chancellor

The Arundell family home at Lanherne near Newquay in Cornwall.

and Cardinal and years of service as the counsellor and friend of King Henry VIII.

The Marquess of Dorset, thanks to his mother's schemes and promotions, was one of England's richest peers. He had fifteen children in all, including a daughter Elizabeth[4] who married Sir John Arundell of Lanherne. She died in 1503[5] when Thomas was very young but there must have been a memory in the family of their connection with Wolsey. It was expected that anyone going up to London to start a career would report to Wolsey and he would remember old favours. Thus Thomas duly made contact and in 1516 he became a gentleman usher in Wolsey's household. He served him faithfully for the rest of the cardinal's life.

When Thomas the Founder began his career, he was perhaps more conscious of his royal connections than the family's friendship with Wolsey. First there was the descent from Edward IV's queen that made him a distant cousin of the King, Henry VIII[6] – this was important in an age which took such things seriously. Indeed, Thomas's grandson,

at the end of the century, reminded Queen Elizabeth I in a letter from
the prison where she had thrown him, that they were both descended
from the womb of Elizabeth Woodville. His aunt Elizabeth of York had
been the beloved wife of Henry VII who had died in 1503, amid general
grief. His Grey grandfather who owned land in sixteen counties had
died in 1501 but his uncle Thomas Grey, Wolsey's one-time pupil was a
great athlete and jousting friend of the King.

On the Arundell side, his grandfather Thomas had supported
the Lancastrians in the Civil Wars along with his Grey grandfather and
when the Duke of Buckingham hatched a conspiracy against the usurper
Richard III in 1483, grandfather Thomas prepared his men in Cornwall
to welcome Henry Tudor's arrival on the south coast from Brittany.
Henry was proclaimed King at Exeter by the Courtenays, supported by
the Marquess of Dorset and grandfather Thomas Arundell. However, the
rising failed, Buckingham was executed at Salisbury and Arundell and
Dorset fled to join Henry Tudor in Brittany where they remained for two
years. At the Cathedral in Rennes at High Mass in 1483, they promised
to recognise Henry as their rightful King. It is not surprising therefore
that the Arundells' men joined Henry when he landed at Milford Haven
in August 1485[7] and marched with him to the Battle of Bosworth. At the
battle, grandfather Thomas Arundell took an arrow in his chest that was
intended for Henry Tudor and he died a few weeks later. There could not
be any greater proof of loyalty to the new dynasty or a better foundation
for a network of useful connections.

Thomas's role in Wolsey's household was to be a gentleman of his
Privy Chamber. The household was magnificent with over 500 people
from a Lord Chamberlain down to cooks and grooms. When in London
Wolsey lived at Bridewell or York Place but his favourite residence was
Hampton Court which he leased from the Knights of St John in 1514 and
proceeded to rebuild as a palace. Wolsey himself, dressed in the scarlet
or crimson of a cardinal, made every journey an impressive procession.
He always carried an orange filled with 'vinegar and other confections

against the pestilent airs' and always there was borne before him the Great Seal of England and his cardinal's hat.[8]

When Thomas arrived in London in about 1516, Wolsey had almost reached the zenith of his power. He was Bishop of Lincoln, Archbishop of York, Cardinal and Lord Chancellor; only the title of Legate for Life remained to be added by the Pope in 1518. His income was said to be over £9,500 a year (£5 million by 2010 values), making him the King's wealthiest subject. But Wolsey's power came not so much from his titles but from his understanding of the psychology of the new King, Henry VIII. When other councillors nagged Henry to apply himself to business and presented alternative policies for his consideration, Wolsey told the King he would do all his business for him as the King 'was not caring to toil in the busy affairs of this realm.' Wolsey was energetic, efficient and totally dedicated to the King. Every day he went to Westminster Hall and the Star Chamber, 'where he spared neither high or low but judged every man whatever his dignity, according to his merits.' Some called him the second King.

There are no clear records of what exactly Thomas Arundell was required to do for Wolsey but the fact that he belonged to his Privy Chamber indicates that he had the closest and most constant access to the Cardinal. He appears to have handled Wolsey's household bills and become his treasurer and later his Latin secretary. He was a close friend of Henry Percy, son of the earl of Northumberland whose relationship with Anne Boleyn was ended on Wolsey's instructions so that she would be available for the King. Wolsey assumed that Anne would be another mistress, not a wife. One letter that survives from 1528 is from Thomas Cromwell to Thomas Arundell, asking him to obtain Wolsey's instructions for his new colleges at Oxford and Ipswich.[9]

Wolsey liked nothing better than a magnificent display. Thomas found it a great struggle to keep up. In several of the eleven letters to his father that survive,[10] he complains about his lack of adequate clothing. Unfortunately they do not carry the date of the year:

22 September ... I am so short of clothes that I stayed with Lady Stanop when my Lord rode from London to Hamtun Court. I am so bare of apparel that I do not cum ne my Lord. I have no more gowns but a pere sersnet[11] I bought this summer and I should be in velvet every day.

Money was short to pay a servant too, but he tells his father that he is looking for a new man, 'ryght tall and honest, dylygent and when I lacke money, to leve me.' Several of the letters deal with family business and the all important issue of marriage. There are proposals for sister Jane but when his father suggests a marriage for him with Lady Oxford's niece, he replies: 'Lady Oxford is as obstinate as a mule. If her niece is similar I had rather go to ruin than have her as my wife'; then he adds that the King has been at Richmond, 'which has emptied my purse and wearied my body.'

A courtier's life was hard; waiting, watching, hoping to be noticed, keeping out of trouble, seizing opportunities. There was no pay, only prospects. Making connections, doing favours was the name of the game. But it was the surest way to travel the road to rank and riches.

During the early years of his service to Wolsey, Thomas had the excitement of participating in the most famous and expensive peace conference in European history, known as the Field of Cloth of Gold, a typical Wolsey extravaganza. Henry came to the throne in 1509 at the age of seventeen, anxious to play a major role on the European stage. In June 1513 he crossed to France and at vast expenditure, captured the towns of Therouanne and Tournai.[12] Henry saw himself as a great Warrior King in the mould of his namesake Henry V but Wolsey feared the cost of such adventures. When Pope Leo X proposed an international peace treaty in 1517, as a prelude to a crusade against the Turks, Wolsey masterminded the Treaty of London between France and England and

*Back view of the Westminster Chasuble showing early 16th century emblems and
the Burgundian orphrey given to Westminster Abbey by Margaret of Burgundy in
1480.*

suggested a meeting between the two kings to celebrate and cement their new friendship.

So it was that Wolsey organised the Field of Cloth of Gold in June 1520. The meetings of the two kings, planned with meticulous attention to detail, took place over two weeks in fields between the English town of Guines, six miles from Calais and the nearby French town of Ardres. Temporary palaces were built with stone foundations, but canvas for the walls and roofs, all decorated with many-coloured tapestries and hangings. The King took a retinue of 3,997 men, Queen Catherine had 1,175 and Wolsey 50 gentlemen (including Thomas Arundell), 12 chaplains and 237 servants. It was in fact a two week long festival of music, food, wine and jousting. The Venetian ambassador wrote perceptively: 'But they hate each other, cordially.' The climax was on Saturday 23 June when Wolsey sang a solemn Mass in the tented chapel, assisted by four cardinals and twenty bishops and watched by three Kings (the King of Navarre had joined in) and three Queens (the Queen Mother of France was the third). For this service and others, Wolsey had borrowed vestments from Westminster Abbey and one of them, which he perhaps wore for this special Mass, is the chasuble now at Wardour.[13]

This provenance is controversial but one account is that Wolsey asked Thomas Arundell, by now his treasurer, to return the chasuble to the Abbey after the festivities but Thomas 'forgot' and it came eventually to Wardour. The superb vestment is decorated with Tudor symbols: Henry's portcullis representing the Beaufort family, Tudor roses, Catherine's personal symbol, the pomegranate and the French fleurs-de-lis to remind the French that Henry also had a claim to be King of France. No more potent symbol of Henry's power survives.[14] At the centre of the chasuble is an orphrey made in Burgundy in the 1470s and given to Westminster Abbey in 1480 by Margaret of Burgundy, Edward IV's sister, when she visited England.[15] The significance of this orphrey which also shows the arms of the Duke of Burgundy impaling the royal arms of England, might have been to remind the French that England was already a respectable European power with important alliances. Whatever the true story, it is difficult other than by involving Thomas, to understand how a vestment from Westminster Abbey, decorated with royal symbols, came to be at Wardour.[16] The Abbey has never held sales of its surplus vestments. The chasuble was not one of the vestments bought in Italy by Father Thorpe for the new chapel in the 1770s. It was never in Italy.

Throughout the early 1520s, Thomas was learning and growing in influence at Wolsey's court. But all was shattered by the problem of the King's marriage and his love affair with Anne Boleyn. The King prided himself on his loyalty to the Church. In 1521 he wrote a reply to the criticisms of the Church by the troublesome German friar, Martin Luther, and defended the seven sacraments in *Assertio Septem Sacramentorum*. In gratitude, Pope Leo X conferred on Henry the title of Defender of the Faith. Five years later, Henry was troubled by personal problems. Queen Catherine, age 41 had failed to give birth to a son who survived and Henry began to believe that this was God's punishment for his decision in 1509 to marry his brother Arthur's widow, a marriage against canon law. Although the Pope had sent a dispensation to overcome the problem, Henry believed it was not in the Pope's power to change the law.

In addition, Henry had fallen in love with Anne Boleyn, a lady-in-waiting who refused to be his mistress and held out for the status of wife. The King consulted Wolsey at an early stage and assumed that he would find a solution, as he always did. It was not unknown for the Pope to issue an annulment of a marriage. Henry asked Wolsey to obtain this on the grounds that it was not within the Pope's power to grant a dispensation and that Catherine's marriage to Arthur had been properly consummated and therefore her second marriage was illegal. Wolsey made various investigations and expected that the Pope would grant him the power to annul the marriage. But in May 1527 a further complication occurred. The armies of Catherine's nephew, the Emperor

Charles V, took the Pope prisoner. The Pope became Charles's puppet. There was no possibility now that he would allow the Pope to deprive his aunt Catherine of her title as Queen of England.

In the spring of 1528 the Pope issued orders for a special court to hear the case in London, presided over by Wolsey and Cardinal Campeggio. Thomas Arundell was given the task of collecting evidence for the King. A major issue was the proof of whether Catherine's marriage to Prince Arthur in 1503 had really been consummated or not. Catherine said 'No' (therefore the dispensation was irrelevant and her second marriage was perfectly legal). Henry tried to prove that it was 'Yes' (and so a dispensation was needed but was invalid and his marriage was illegal). Perhaps it was Thomas Arundell who interviewed Sir Anthony Willoughby, one of Arthur's body servants and reported that Arthur had said to him, on the morning after his first night with Catherine, 'bring me a cup of ale, for I have been this night in the midst of Spayne.'[17]

In any case,

The last page of a long letter from Thomas Arundell to Cardinal Wolsey on 17 October 1530, warning him about his enemies at Court and promising that he had spoken to the Duke of Norfolk on Wolsey's behalf.

Thomas Arundell is recorded as one of the officers in charge of the King's Evidence when the court opened at Blackfriars on 31 May 1529. The king had built a new palace at Blackfriars and the court proceedings took place in a building belonging to the Dominican Priory next to the palace. Thomas Arundell must have heard Queen Catherine make her stirring appeal to the King: 'Sir, I beseech you for all the love that hath been between us and for the love of God, let me have justice and right . . . when ye had me at the first I was a true maid without touch of man.'[18]

On the 31 July 1529 the Court was adjourned and the Pope withdrew the case to Rome. The King was frustrated and impatient. Wolsey was blamed and his career was finished. He limped on but in October the Great Seal was taken away from him and he retired to his house at Esher to await the King's pleasure. It was at this time that he wrote: 'in this my calamity . . . I would gladly have Arundell here with me'[19] and there were reports that he had to borrow from Thomas, 'dishes to eat his meat in and plate to drink in and also linen clothes to make use of.'[20] Eventually the King stripped Wolsey of most of his offices and ordered him to go to York to look after his archdiocese there. Thomas remained at court and did his best to intercede for his old master. A letter survives from him to Wolsey dated 17 October 1530.[21] He reports that he had met the Duke of Norfolk and tried to persuade him that Wolsey had no ambition left; and also he had tried to intercede with the Lord Chancellor and Chief

The 2nd Duke of Norfolk, Margaret Arundell's grandfather who was the richest and most powerful peer in England. (reproduced by kind permission of His Grace the Duke of Norfolk: The Courtauld)

Justice on Wolsey's behalf. The Duke, always an enemy of Wolsey, had been unsympathetic and said he knew Wolsey was scheming to get back his power and authority. It was almost the end. On 4 November Wolsey was arrested on a charge of High Treason and ordered to make his way to London for trial and probable execution. He died at Leicester Abbey on 25 November 1530.

What happened to Thomas Arundell? He was determined to capitalise on the years of training he had received in Wolsey's household. His time had come. He was a friend of the king's new minister, Thomas Cromwell from their days together in Wolsey's household. On 11 November 1529 the King chose Thomas Arundell, personally, to be Sheriff of Somerset and Dorset. The Arundells owned land in both counties which had come to them with the marriage in 1451 of Thomas's great grandfather to Katherine Chideock. Thomas made his home at Symondsbury Manor near Chideock.[22]

Thomas, 3rd Duke of Norfolk by Holbein. He was Margaret Arundell's uncle and was saved from execution only by the death of Henry VIII.
(reproduced by kind permission of His Grace the Duke of Norfolk: The Courtauld)

In December 1530 came Thomas's splendid marriage to Margaret Howard, daughter of Lord Edmund Howard and granddaughter of the second Duke of Norfolk.[23] The Howards were the most powerful non-royal family in the land. Margaret's grandfather Thomas had led the army that defeated the Scots at Flodden in 1513 and in 1520 Henry named him, Guardian of England. Her uncle the 3rd Duke had a long career as Lord High Treasurer and defeated the threat from the

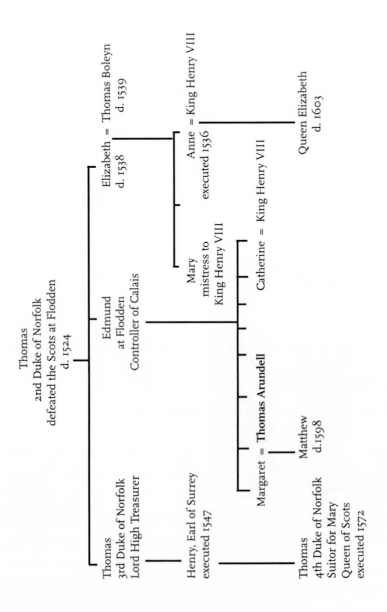

Thomas Arundell and the Howard Family

Pilgrimage of Grace in 1536. He made a disastrous mistake in the last weeks of Henry's reign that led to six years in the Tower. Later in 1540, Margaret's sister Catherine became Queen of England as Henry's fifth wife and so for a few months, Thomas was the King's brother-in-law. Not bad for a young man from Cornwall.

We next hear of Thomas in May 1533 when he assisted at the coronation of Anne Boleyn. Henry had married her, secretly and bigamously, in January 1533 when she was already pregnant. The coronation took place on 1 June in Westminster Abbey preceded by many days of elaborate ceremonies. Cranmer, the new Archbishop of Canterbury, had annulled the King's marriage to Catherine, on his own authority on 23 May, rather late in the day. The coronation was as magnificent as Henry could make it, with processions from the Tower to Westminster and Anne in a chariot covered with cloth of silver. Thomas had been made a Knight of the Bath on the previous evening along with seventeen other courtiers. They all joined the procession, 'ridinge in blewe gowns with hoodes on their shoulders.'[24] At the coronation in Westminster Abbey, Anne was anointed and crowned Queen with her grandmother, the old Duchess of Norfolk 'bearing up her train.' At the banquet that evening in Westminster Hall, Thomas Arundell was 'Carver for the ladies at the board' and cupbearer for Archbishop Cranmer.

What did Thomas make of all these changes? We simply do not know. In the spring of 1534 Parliament passed the Act of Supremacy, making the King and not the Pope Head of the Church in England. But Henry himself was conservative in religious beliefs and wanted the new Church of England to retain all the doctrines and rituals of the Catholic Church. Thomas probably accepted this and regarded the break with Rome as a temporary estrangement for political reasons. The church needed reforms and perhaps he accepted the dissolution of the monasteries in the later 1530s under that heading. But at court there were other people who urged doctrinal reforms. They supported a denial of the real presence in the Mass and demanded justification by faith and clerical marriage. Henry would have none of this and in his Act of Six Articles of 1539 he re-affirmed all the Catholic beliefs and traditions. Naturally, the court was increasingly divided. Thomas Arundell always sided with the traditionalists against the reformers.

In practical terms, Thomas was about to amass the wealth that laid the foundations of Arundell family fortunes for the next five centuries. His old friend Thomas Cromwell, now Vicar-General of the Church, made him in 1536 First Receiver of the Court of Augmentations for Cornwall,

Portrait of a youthful Henry VIII on the Letters Patent granting Thomas Arundell some of the estates of Shaftesbury Abbey in 1541.

Devon, Dorset and Somerset. His job was to supervise the dissolution of the monasteries in those counties, administer the land and buildings and transfer them to the King. It was the most profound change in land ownership since the Norman Conquest.It would have been surprising if the occupant of such a post had not taken the opportunity to feather his own nest. Such has been the custom of men in power throughout history and in all countries. The Benedictine Abbey of Shaftesbury was the oldest and richest foundation for women in the land. Catherine of Aragon stayed there in 1501 on her way to London to marry Prince Arthur. In 1538 the residents were an abbess and 57 nuns, including Wolsey's daughter. Despite appeals to Cromwell to allow the abbey to remain open, it closed on 23 March 1539, the last of all the English nunneries to submit.

In 1541 Thomas bought the manors of Tisbury and Dinton from the abbey's estates for £1,761 14s 10½d (£600,000 at 2010 values).[25]

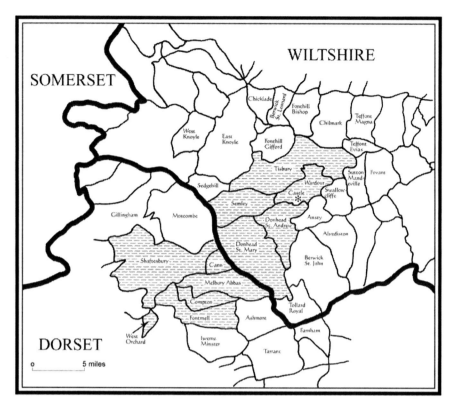

Land acquired by Thomas Arundell in the early 1540s, mainly from the estates of the dissolved Shaftesbury Abbey; more was added later

Three years later he added Donhead St Mary, Donhead St Andrew, Charlton, Combe, Compton, Fontmell and Melbury Abbas for £2,609 1s 1d (£850,000 now). By the time of his execution in 1552, his estates also included ten more manors in the north of Dorset. The younger son had become the richest Arundell in the whole family.

Those years in Wolsey's household had paid a handsome reward. Most of the land was bought from the King but some was a gift, such as indicated by the grant of land under Letters Patent of 1546, 'for the good, true, faithful and acceptable services to us and our most dear consort Catherine done by the said Thomas.' The final purchase was the grand castle at Wardour which Thomas bought in 1547 from the

The earliest known picture of Wardour Castle from a survey for the Earl of Pembroke in 1566.

Greville family. It was in a central position on his new estates, a most extraordinary fortified manor house of hexagonal shape based on French designs.

The early 1540s were good years for the Arundells. In August 1540 the King married Arundell's sister-in-law, Catherine Howard. The marriage has left no record in the family papers unless we assume that the first purchase of monastic property from the King was somehow linked with the closer royal relationship. Margaret's sister was notorious for her sexual promiscuity and the King was appalled when he discovered the details. The marriage lasted only eighteen months. We do not know Margaret's reaction to her sister's execution in February 1542 but it cannot have affected Thomas's position as a favoured courtier because he was appointed Chamberlain to the new Queen, Catherine Parr, in 1543. Thomas and Margaret had five children and spent their time between Symondsbury, Wardour and London. The King's conservative approach to religious doctrine suited the Arundells and was backed by the Howard family, Bishop Gardiner and many others. The reformers made little headway and all was well with the world. In the King's Book, issued in 1543, there was almost no change in Catholic doctrine. No one was prepared to rock the boat as the King approached his final years.

Then in December 1546 there was disaster for the conservative group supporting the King. They had been dominant throughout the 1540s. The Duke of Norfolk and his son the Earl of Surrey, were accused of treason and imprisoned in the Tower. Surrey was reported as saying that he and his father would rule the kingdom when the old king died. Surrey displayed a crest with the arms of Edward the Confessor quartered with his own. Only the King was allowed to display those arms. This challenge to royal authority could not be ignored. Surrey, Margaret Arundell's cousin, was executed on 19 January 1547 on Tower Hill. Her uncle, the Duke was saved only by the death of the King. The conservatives were fatally weakened. The King's support of the conservatives had ensured that the reformers would be kept in check. Now, with the prospect of a nine year old boy as the next King and Norfolk's opponents in power, the floodgates of reform would open.

Thomas would need to play his cards cautiously. Long years at court had taught him how to navigate the seas of intrigue and deceit but perhaps it would be safer to stay in Wiltshire in his new castle.

By late December 1546, the King was obviously dying. He could move around his palace at Whitehall only on a chair propelled by wheels. He had a 54 inch waist. He saw neither the Queen nor his children. The men who attended him in his Privy Chamber held enormous power to arrange the succession. They were Sir William Paget, the King's Secretary; Sir Anthony Denny and Sir William Herbert (from Wilton), both Gentlemen of the Privy Chamber. They were all strong reformers. The conservative group was in disarray. Prince Edward's uncle, Edward Seymour, led a reform group that was desperate for power – men such as Dudley and Seymour's brother Thomas. Seymour was heard talking secretly outside the king's room with Paget who promised he would arrange things 'as required'. The mechanism Paget used was the King's will.

Prince Edward was a boy of only nine. Obviously he could not govern on his own but would need a council to act for him. The King made his will on 30 December 1546. It should have been stamped immediately with the dry stamp – a wooden block carved with Henry's signature which left an impression on the parchment that was later inked in. We know that Paget and his friends forged Henry's will because the signature was not recorded in the schedule of signings until 27 January 1547, the day before Henry died and details of the will were changed to make it possible for Edward Seymour to be chosen as Lord Protector. Not only that, but as soon as Henry died at 2 a.m. on 28 January, holding Cranmer's hand, Paget announced that he had found an extra clause of the will on a piece of paper in the King's pocket. This contained a list of names of leading men whom Henry wanted to reward with titles (one duke, one marquess, four earls and ten barons). Thomas Arundell's name was one of those to be made a baron. Henry also wished to distribute land to these men so they would have the status for their new positions. But Paget then announced that the King had crossed out certain names, including Thomas Arundell's and other conservatives' and he must make sure the King's true wishes were carried out. Seymour was made Duke of Somerset and Lord Protector, Dudley, Earl of Warwick and lands worth £3,200 a year were distributed to their supporters. There was nothing for Thomas Arundell.

The writing was on the wall. Without a King to exercise effective power, the next few years would be a period of intense rivalry and intrigue. The government under Seymour launched wholesale religious reforms – charities and Masses for the dead were abolished, statues and shrines and stained glass were destroyed, the Mass was abolished and replaced by Communion, a new Book of Common Prayer was made compulsory . . . Thomas and his friends watched with great anxiety.

In January 1549 Parliament passed an Act of Uniformity to enforce the Book of Common Prayer. In June Thomas's cousin Humphrey, one of the stay-at-home Arundells, launched the Prayer Book Rebellion in Cornwall and Devon. The rebels demanded a return to the Mass and the Act of Six Articles as laid down by Henry VIII. They said 'we will not receive the new service because it is but like a Christmas game.' Thomas tried to distance himself but the Arundells never recovered from the association of rebellion with their name. Sir John at Lanherne claimed he was sick when Lord Russell, charged with destroying the

A contemporary engraving of the execution of the Duke of Somerset on 22 January 1552 on Tower Hill. Thomas Arundell was executed 35 days later in the same place.

rebels, asked him for his presence with 200 men. This hesitation would be remembered against the Arundells for a long time.

In October 1549, Somerset was sent to the Tower after a seizure of power by his rival Dudley, Earl of Warwick. For a short time it looked as if Thomas was about to triumph. He supported Dudley and hoped for a place in the new government. The Imperial ambassador reported to the Emperor: 'Thomas Arundell, a good man and of the old faith . . . he was the prime instrument in uniting the Lords against the Protector.'[26] Dudley promised him the post of Comptroller to the King as reward for his opposition to Somerset but then changed his mind and blocked the appointment. He chose reformers as his fellow councillors. Thomas had backed the wrong horse.

In January 1550 Thomas was put under house arrest but then Somerset was released from the Tower so that the charges against him would not drag down Dudley (now Duke of Northumberland) as well. Arundell was soon released too but made a fatal mistake, hard to understand in one who had a lifetime's experience of navigating court

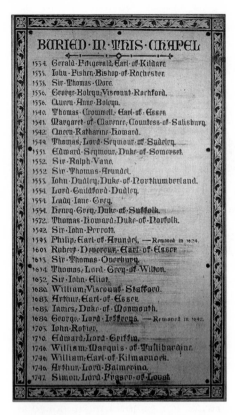

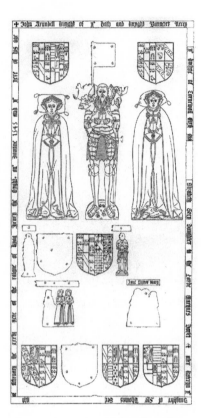

Left: Plaque in the Chapel Royal of St. Peter ad Vincula in the Tower of London, recording the burial there of Thomas Arundell and other members of his family Right: Brass plate on the floor of St. Columb Major Church, Cornwall, showing the small figure of Thomas Arundell in armour, appropriately missing his head; from a drawing in 1890 by Roscoe Gibbs.

intrigue. He believed Somerset when he said that he was prepared to abandon religious reforms, return to the old ways and work together. Thomas appears to have lost his sense of judgment. Why did he take his eye off the ball at this crucial moment? He agreed to help Somerset, his old enemy, plan a seizure of power from Northumberland. If only he had retired to Wardour and country pursuits. The result was that when Somerset was arrested again, on 14 October 1551, on suspicion of plotting to overthrow the government, Thomas was arrested again too, charged with treason and sent to the Tower. The council interrogated him on 21 October and he said as he left: 'Neither I nor any of my family has ever been a traitor but all of you know who has.' He looked at Northumberland as he left the room.

In December 1551 Somerset was put on trial in Westminster Hall. The crowds cried 'God Save the Duke' but he was found guilty of felony, not treason and sentenced to be beheaded. On 27 January 1552 Thomas and three others were found guilty of conspiracy. The jury was reluctant to convict them 'but locked in a room together from noon until the following morning without food or water, they eventually submitted.'[27] With three other prisoners, Thomas was beheaded on Tower Hill on the morning of 26 February 1552. He declared his innocence of any wrongdoing. Henry Mackyn, a merchant, wrote in his diary, 'their bodies were put into different new coffins to be buried and their heads in to the Tower in cases and there buried too.'[28] In 1876 their bodies were reburied in the crypt of the Chapel of St. Peter ad Vincula.

All the Arundell estates were forfeited to the Crown as was the custom. They were worth £641 13s 4¼d a year, more than those of many earls. Wardour Castle became the property of the Earl of Pembroke but just before Margaret Arundell died at Shaftesbury in 1571 it was re-possessed by her son in exchange for some land. None of this generation of Arundells could have believed that the there would still be Arundells at Wardour nearly 500 years later.

2

Thomas the Valiant

THOMAS the Valiant is the first Arundell we can see as well as hear. He was painted in miniature by George Gower in 1585 and again as an old man by Van Dyck in 1630. Both pictures are still at Wardour.[1] Thomas was born in 1559[2] and named after the grandfather he never knew.

Few Elizabethans were better connected to people of power and influence. He was a distant cousin of the Queen through his grandmother Margaret Howard. But more significant to him and perhaps to the Queen was that they were both descended from Elizabeth Woodville, the wife of Edward IV.[3] His mother, Margaret Willoughby came from one of the richest gentry families in the Midlands and served the Queen as maid of honour and then as lady-in-waiting for 26 years. She knew Elizabeth intimately in all her unpredictable moods. His father Matthew spent long years at Court and retired to Wardour only in the 1570s when he started to modernise the old castle and employed Robert Smythson to introduce the new classical style.

Thomas spent his early years in London, partly because his parents were at Court but also because the castle at Wardour was still in the hands of Lord Pembroke after the attainder and execution of his grandfather. In 1579 Thomas went on a sort of GAP year tour of Europe. It is usually thought that the reason was an attempt to escape punishment for opposing the religious policies of the government. A Victorian

Thomas 1st Lord Arundell in old age, an engraving based on a portrait by Van Dyck from the early 1630s.

antiquarian wrote that he was 'committed to prison by Queen Elizabeth in the summer of 1580 for his zeal in the Catholic cause'⁴ but no evidence of this has been found. However, there is a copy in the family archives of the letter from Elizabeth to the Holy Roman Emperor, Rudolf II in 1579, commending Thomas on his travels and describing him as her beloved kinsman, 'of the same blood'.⁵ We have no information about the places Thomas visited on his tour or the people he met, except that he made contact with the Duke of Guise in Paris. The Duke was the first cousin of

Mary Queen of Scots and head of her French family. Many believed that Mary had a stronger claim to the throne of England than Elizabeth so anyone who made contact with Mary was suspected of treason. We know about this contact because Thomas, many years later, reminded James I that he had been sympathetic to his mother, Mary Queen of Scots and offered his services to her via the Duke, in Paris in 1580.[6] However, Walsingham, Elizabeth's spymaster, discovered this disloyalty in 1580 and Thomas was banished from court for thirteen months.

On 18 June 1585, in the chapel attached to Southampton House in London, he married Mary Wriothesley, daughter of the second Earl of Southampton. Her family ran parallel to the Arundells in rising to fame and fortune under the Tudor monarchs.[7] Her grandfather was Secretary to Henry VIII in 1540 and later Lord Chancellor. The reward was 5000 acres of the Titchfield Abbey estate in Hampshire. The Wriothesleys were, like the Arundells, conservative in religious matters and by 1585 could be described as definitely Catholic. The brightest star was Mary's brother Henry, the third earl. Lord Burghley was his guardian; he was strikingly handsome and was painted more times than any other of Elizabeth's subjects. He is famous as the friend and patron of Shakespeare in the 1590s.

Mary Wriothesley was a good wife to Thomas and there were three children of the marriage. Unfortunately she quarrelled with her father-in-law and was banned from Wardour. In a letter to Robert Cecil on 23 June 1597 Matthew Arundell complains about Mary, 'from whom in spite of many services rendered, I have received too many indignities to write of; so much so that I have protested I will never live in one house with her during my life time.'[8]

When the Armada crisis erupted in 1588, Thomas gave £100 for the defence of England and opposed the Pope's Declaration, renewing the Bull of Excommunication which called on all Catholics to unite in overthrowing Elizabeth, 'that infamous, depraved, accursed heretic'. What sort of Catholic was Thomas? David Lunn described his father as 'a wait-and-see' Catholic and Thomas as 'a fully-fledged Counter-Reformation recusant.'[9] But the evidence is that he followed his father's lead in trying to be both a loyal Catholic and a patriotic Englishman. He was walking a tightrope. Although he was imprisoned several times in the 1590s under suspicion of sheltering Catholic priests, there is, on the other side, his astonishing decision to take the Oath of Allegiance on 12 June 1610, four years after he was ennobled and to play a full part in Jacobean politics. He attended Parliament 186 times in the following 20 years and sat on many committees of peers. Many Catholics found it impossible to take the Oath because of its reference to the Pope's heretical beliefs about deposing monarchs.[10] Thomas obviously did not.

Thomas's chief claim to fame is his seizure of the Turkish flag at the Battle of Gran in 1595 and the enraged reaction of Elizabeth when she discovered he had accepted the title of Count of the Holy Roman Empire from the Emperor Rudolf II. There were many ways to make a name for oneself in Elizabeth England – service to the Queen, voyages of discovery, winning military victories, but one unusual and guaranteed method was to produce a temper tantrum from the Queen, so violent that she issued one of her declarations, full of memorable words and phrases, that would be forever associated with the name of the recipient. Such was the dubious honour won by Thomas. But why did he go to fight for the Holy Roman Emperor in 1595 on the

The Emperor Rudolf from an engraving of 1603.

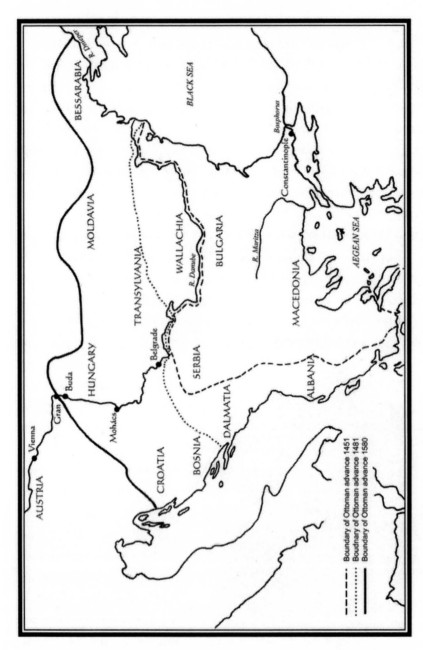

Map of Europe showing the Turkish advance towards Vienna and the fortress of Gran on the river Danube.

banks of the Danube? It might seem that his father engineered it so that he would escape the bad company of the Southampton set in London, (Shakespeare and all his friends). The real reason was that he was being used by the Queen in the devious game of international politics.

He left Leigh on Sea on 4 June 1595, taking with him the same letter of introduction to the Holy Roman Emperor that Elizabeth had given him sixteen years previously. We now need to look briefly at European politics to understand what lay behind Thomas's journey to fight on the Danube.

The Ottoman Empire stretched from the borders of Persia in the east to the River Danube in the west. Suleiman the Magnificent (ruled 1520-1566), a contemporary of Henry VIII, led the expansion of the Muslim empire to its greatest extent. He fought thirteen major military campaigns and eleven of those were in the west. In 1526 his army crossed the Danube and defeated the King of Hungary at the battle of Mohacs, one of the decisive battles of the world. Europe lay open to the Muslim soldiers. In 1529 Suleiman's army besieged Vienna but he had to withdraw after 29 days because of the onset of winter.[11] The Turks were the enemy who kept Christian children awake in their beds at night. Stories abounded in Europe of those most inhuman barbarians, the most savage enemies of the True Faith who desecrated churches, burnt libraries and raped women and boys. The Turks were demonized all over Europe.[12]

How did Europe react? Mostly with resolutions of undying hostility to the infidel and promises of support for the Pope's appeal for a crusade – on the surface at least Europe was united. But the story is not as simple as that. In 1566 Suleiman died and his successor made a truce on the European front while he turned his attention to the Persians in the East. The truce lasted for 24 years and enabled the Holy Roman Emperor and the King of Spain, leaders in the defence of Europe, to turn their attention to problems inside Europe. Philip II of Spain decided to solve the problems posed by the Dutch, who wanted freedom from Spanish rule and by the English who wanted freedom from the Catholic Church.

The Armada, launched by Philip in 1588 to invade England and convert its people to the Catholic faith was one result of peace with the Turks and Philip's new freedom to re-arrange his priorities. England survived, thanks to the storms which blew the Spanish ships off course, but by 1593 the situation was threatening again. The Spanish Atlantic fleet had been rebuilt and it was no secret that Philip would soon launch another Armada. He did so in 1596, 1597 and 1598. What should Elizabeth do? It was not surprising if her enthusiasm for the truce with the Ottoman Empire wore thin. Keeping the Habsburgs busy fighting the Turks took the pressure off England. But to be seen to be encouraging the Turks to attack Europe was unthinkable. Elizabeth therefore played a devious double game. Secretly, she negotiated with the Sultan for him to launch another war along the river Danube. Rumours abounded that she was a traitor to Christendom. Elizabeth denied them vehemently. Publicly and proudly she sent a brave young courtier, Thomas Arundell, to fight side by side with fellow Christians against the infidel Turks as proof that she was a good European Christian. It is a pity she was not more grateful for his brilliant success.

English friendship with the Ottoman Empire was a recent development. English merchants had long envied the French their links with the fabulously wealthy Empire where the first French Embassy was established in 1534 and a trade treaty made in 1536. In 1543 the Ottoman fleet had wintered in the French port of Toulon, so strong was their friendship. France was deaf to appeals for Christian solidarity against the Muslims. Trade took precedence over the Faith. English merchants lagged far behind but found in Istanbul an insatiable market for tin (to use in the making of bronze cannon), iron, lead, muskets, sword blades and saltpetre. Bernardine de Mendoza, the Spanish ambassador in England wrote to King Philip on 28 November 1579: 'The Turks are also desirous of friendship with the English on account of the tin which has been sent thither for the last few years . . . . . . as they cannot cast their guns without it, whilst the English make a tremendous profit.'[13]

In June 1580 a 'farman' granted English merchants full trading privileges in Turkey. The Levant Company was established in 1581. The first English ambassador, William Harebone, arrived on 29 March 1583 with a letter from Elizabeth, beginning: 'Elizabeth, the most powerful defender of the faith against idolaters sends greetings to Mahommet, the Grand Vizier of the Turks . . . ' She immediately asked for a secret promise that the Turks would attack Spain in the Mediterranean if England attacked Spain in the Atlantic. This was agreed but deeds were slow to match words. The next ambassador, Edward Barton continued to promote the plan and wrote to Elizabeth in 1588: 'In my small judgment, I think it is nothing offensive to God to set one of his enemies against the other, the Infidel against the Idolater, to the end that while they are by the ears, God's people might respite and take strength.'[14] The Sultan praised the Protestant destruction of religious idols and admitted that Turkish military pressure on the Habsburgs had ensured the survival of the Protestants.

In 1587, with preparations almost complete for the Spanish invasion of England, Elizabeth appealed again to the Sultan. She told him in secret letters that he was the greatest of all the princes of this world, 'for the express purpose of destroying idolaters' and that King Philip of Spain was 'head of all idolaters, our common accursed enemy'. Spain intended to destroy England and then 'when no other obstacle shall remain in Christendom, the Spaniard will direct his invincible strength to the destruction of thee and thy empire'. She appealed to the Sultan to make war, 'so the proud Spaniard and the lying Pope will not only have the Cup of promised Victory dashed from their lips but will receive the punishment in their own person due to their rashness'. However, no practical help came from the Sultan at this time and Elizabeth denied she had asked for any.

In 1593 there was tension along the Danube border between the Habsburg and Ottoman empires. Guerrilla warfare broke out and might easily escalate. This was manna from heaven for Elizabeth as she waited for another Spanish invasion. But on the surface she played the usual game. She wrote to the English ambassador in Prague on 14 April 1593 instructing him to offer the Holy Roman Emperor the services of the English ambassador in Istanbul, to persuade the Sultan to hold back from attacks along the Danube that he was rumoured to be preparing. In return, she asked the Emperor to deny publicly the libels published by the Catholic Church all over Europe that she was encouraging the Turks to attack Christendom. As proof of her good faith she arranged for her brave, young kinsman, Thomas Arundell, to join the Emperor's army. All Europe would witness her solidarity with the Emperor and her defence of Christian Europe. What was known to only a few people was that when the Emperor Mehmed III marched north with a great army to attack Christian Europe, two years later in 1595, the English ambassador in Istanbul, Edward Barton, was travelling secretly with him to provide assistance. Elizabeth was having her cake and eating it.

The fortress of Gran, now named Esztergom, was captured by the Turks in 1543. It is 60 miles south east of Vienna on a bend in the Danube and its capture secured for the Turks control of Hungary and a significant advance towards the heart of Christian Europe. Thomas Arundell left England in June 1595 and arrived in Gran just as the siege reached a crucial stage. The details of what happened next are not clear

A Victorian painting of the capture of the Turkish standard by Thomas Arundell at the fortress of Gran in 1595.

but one version has it that on 7 September 1595 he scaled a tower, seized the Turkish flag and replaced it with the Imperial standard. This caused such a collapse of morale among the Turks that they abandoned the castle. So sudden a surrender had rarely happened before in Turkish military exploits. Thomas's own version is more dramatic.[15] He suddenly broke from the front line of the Imperial army, hewed down six Turks with his sabre and wrested the great standard of their Prophet out of the hands of the seventh and passed it to Rudolf's general. Despite being dangerously wounded, he carried on fighting and the Turkish forces melted away as they knew the castle was lost.[16]

Meanwhile, the Sultan was campaigning in Hungary and in October 1596 he won a great victory at Mezökeresztes and re-asserted Ottoman control over south-eastern Europe. But Thomas's capture of the standard enabled the Habsburgs to claim a great victory for Christian Europe too and Elizabeth to claim part of the credit.

The helmet that Thomas wore is now in the chancel of Tisbury Church as part of a memorial to the last Lord Arundell.[17] The Keeper of Armour in the Royal Armouries has commented that the helmet was made in Germany between 1555 and 1560 and therefore could have been worn by Thomas but the plates attached to the bottom of the helmet at front and back are made from an infantry pikeman's gorget of the period 1625 to

The helmet in Tisbury church worn by Thomas Arundell at the Battle of Gran.

1630, so the whole helmet as now displayed could not have been worn by Thomas. The spike at the top was added to carry a funerary crest made of wood which has disappeared. Before a helmet was hung in a church this was usually added to identify the owner.

Soon after the victory at Gran, the Emperor Rudolf decided to reward Thomas with the title of Count of the Holy Roman Empire. The warrant for this was issued on 14 December 1595 at the royal palace in

Prague[18] and gave Thomas a seat in the Imperial Diet, enabled him to purchase land and raise troops in the Empire and most importantly descended to all his heirs both male and female. It was not an empty reward. There had been a few precedents for English subjects receiving foreign titles, the last in 1499 when Sir Robert Gurson went to fight the Turks under the banner of Emperor Maximilian I and received a similar honour. Henry VII did not regard it as a problem and Gurson was accepted at Court.

The seal of the Emperor Rudolf on the Grant giving Thomas Arundell the title of Count of the Holy Roman Empire.

But there was a very different monarch 100 years later. Elizabeth exploded in rage when she heard about the title and ordered Thomas to be thrown into the Fleet prison. Her reasons were that such a title must indicate a secret allegiance between the recipient and donor; such a link betrayed Thomas's loyalty and service to his sovereign and upset English noblemen who would feel themselves upstaged. There was no gratitude for the fact that Thomas provided his Queen with a diplomatic trump card, enabling her to claim that she stood at the front of the anti-Muslim crusade.

The Queen's anger, as usual, was quickly translated into memorable words. William Camden, the Westminster schoolmaster writing in the early 17th century and using the Queen's and ministers' archives, gives us the best version:

> As chaste women ought not to cast their eyes upon any other than their own husbands, so neither ought subjects to cast their eyes upon

any other prince than him whom God hath set over them. I would not have my sheep branded with another man's mark; I would not have them follow the whistle of a strange shepherd.[19]

Fortunately, we can trace the process of punishment and negotiation that Thomas experienced by using the Cecil family papers preserved at Hatfield House. There are 38 letters between June 1595 and August 1600 dealing with the Arundell problem. They were written by the Arundell family to Robert Cecil who became Elizabeth's Secretary of State in 1596, the omnipresent royal servant whom she called 'my little man'. Thomas calls Cecil his 'cousin and kinsman' but it has not been possible to discover the genetic source of this relationship.[20] Some of the letters refer to Lord Burghley, Robert Cecil's father who was the Queen's Lord Treasurer until his death in 1598. The letters give us only Thomas's side of the story so we have to imagine the Queen's and Cecil's replies, now lost. Unfortunately there are too many letters to quote from more than a few and the progress of the dispute is confused by enquiries into Thomas's role as a Catholic who refused to attend the services of the Church of England. He was also suspected of harbouring 'Massing priests'. Over the period of five years Thomas was imprisoned on three occasions, banned from Court three times and sent down to Wardour twice to be 'overlooked' by his father. During some of the time at home he lived in Ansty Manor as his father refused to have Thomas's wife under his own roof.

The first letter[21] about the title is dated 1 February 1596 from Ivybridge[22] in Devon, from Thomas Arundell to Robert Cecil:

Had I not suffered a shipwreck and so lost all my apparel, linen, horses, money and whatsoever else I had and withal gotten an extreme cold by tumbling into the sea, for the safety of my life, I would myself have been the deliverer of these salutations. I understand of divers bad reports raised of me since my departure but I have neither been

at Rome nor had to do with any of the Popish or Spanish factions . . .
I have a letter of the Emperor to Her Majesty . . .

Six days later the explosion occurred. The Queen was at Richmond and had had a sleepless night. Soon after 8 o'clock she sent a message to Lord Cobham, her Lord Chamberlain, that he was to contact Lord Burghley and tell him to find Thomas Arundell and throw him into the Fleet prison. She was much offended that he had accepted an honour from the Emperor without her permission. She ordered Burghley to get hold of the patent, read it carefully and make a list of all previous recipients of foreign titles. He found only five.

From prison on 3 March Thomas wrote a long letter to Cecil:

As for the Emperor's message it is this: that he is glad to hear so strong proofs that Her Majesty is not in league with the Turk; that he was ever willing of himself to think so, though some would have persuaded him otherwise — But lest I forget myself, having been in a manner a close prisoner this long time, even to the prejudice of my health, I do in all humility expect the gracious censure of her never erring judgment in whose blissful favour stands the total sum of my earthly happiness.

At this point the Queen decided she must write directly to the Emperor about her concerns. Her long letter is a masterpiece of balanced diplomatic communication, summarised here in 21st century language:

The Queen to the Emperor
I received your letter dated 30 December only on 6 March because Thomas Arundell was shipwrecked and forced to swim to save his life.
I've heard rumours that Thomas is pretending to have a title, Earl of the Empire. It's very strange, I can't believe it.

He's lost the grant of title in the sea.

So, he says he's come home as an earl when he left as a private gentleman without any title.

No subject of my kingdom has been treated like this before by any other King or Emperor in Christendom. He'll have to do service to you but he's bound by birth to serve me with his life, blood, lands, goods and all his earthly power.

I was very angry and refused to receive him; its upset my noblemen who feel slighted. I've put him in prison and he's confessed his error.

But I know you've got lots of goodwill towards me and he's done service against the common enemy of Christ. You were really kind to take him on my recommendation but you've gone over the top in rewarding him.

So, all I can do is to thank you most heartily for your kindness. I can see now that this is really a testimony of your love to me.

I'm sure you'll agree with me about all this. I know you have great respect for me as a Sovereign Queen as I do for you.

Let me know if I can do anything for you.

More letters followed from Thomas to Cecil, explaining that he was devastated by the Queen's anger and pointing out that the main effect of her behaviour was to enable people in Europe to say she was pro-Turk. Something must have worked because on 15 April 1596 Thomas was summoned to Lord Burghley and discharged from prison but banned from Court. A few days later he was called back to Cecil to be questioned about his contacts with the Emperor and Spain. His London house was searched and papers seized. In July he decided to pile on his flattery of the Queen with a shovel:

I crave that one kiss of those grace-giving hands may be a confirmation to me of Her Majesty's favours, the enjoying of which I have made the scope of all my life's actions . . . the irresistible force of her virtues may easily overcharge my mind, too weak a vessel for so strong a liquor . . . Hers I am whatsoever I am; her kinsman though unworthy; her subject, her sworn servant; whom God ever direct and prosper, whatsoever become of me or my fortune.

Through all these years of confusion about Thomas's status at Court and his negotiations with Cecil there runs the sub-plot of his relationship with his father. Thomas feared his father had disinherited him. In December 1598 he wrote to Cecil to report that old Sir Matthew was dying at Wardour of a burning ague and intolerable pains of 'stone and strangurye'.[23] On 26 December he wrote from Ansty Manor to report his father's death on 24 December. The following is a modern paraphrase of the letter:

My most worthy, most dear father is dead. He repented the errors of his youth. His last breath ended in the name of Jesus. He loved his friends and his country. He loved his Queen. He left many excessive legacies to the poor. Towards the end he asked about Her Majesty's welfare and prayed daily for her prosperity and victory over her enemies. He left Her Majesty two presents, of little worth:

a little table carpet wrought in China (which he admired but isn't worthy of one so high)

me

I will bring both of these to your hands soon. His land is all tied up in the payment of the legacies so I won't be able to live like a gentleman; and he hasn't left me any goods or the use of them. But he loved me and I was the only one with him at the end and I alone fed him. It's the cunning of some of my enemies that leaves me in the state like this. God's will be done. My last hope is to prostrate myself at the feet of my beloved Queen. She's sent me some really motherly advice.

Despite all his fears of being disinherited, Thomas was left most of his father's property.[24] Sir Matthew's will was long and gives a clue to his character and generosity. He began, 'My Soul to Almighty God and my body to be buried in the parish church of Tysburie.' He left £2,000 (£264,000 in 2010 values), 'whereby the poor of Tysbury, Donhead Andrew, Donhead Marie in co. Wilts and of Melburie, Compton and Fountmell in co. Dorset should be set to work.'[25] The will is then full of bequests of clothes and horses to friends and servants. 'To each of my household servants one year's wages except the two riders who shall have 53s 4d each . . . To the Rt. Hon. Sir Robert Cecil Kt. my horse called Otoman, desiring him to be good to my son for my sake . . .' Christopher Mercer received his 'old furred cloak' and Justice Walmeslowe, 'my gold spectacles'.

Thomas thus found himself the new owner of Wardour Castle, one of the most luxurious fortified tower houses in the country. His father had

lavished great attention and wealth on the property. It was like no other building in England – a hexagonal shape built around a hexagonal courtyard and enclosed by a hexagonal curtain wall. Its only rivals were several royal palaces in Europe. In about 1576, Robert Smythson, then working at Longleat came over to Wardour and was engaged to modernise the castle. He inserted more windows in the castle to give more light – they were arranged symmetrically

Wardour Castle was improved and modernised by Robert Smythson in the 1570s and 1580s when he was working at Longleat.

and in a special Tudor Gothic style so they would harmonise with the medieval castle; he added classical ornamentation on the entrance front and inside the courtyard he built a splendid Doric doorway to the Great Hall; he provided a new drainage system, piped water and lavish installation of privies.

Fortunately, we know a great deal about the contents of the castle at this time. On 10 August 1605 Thomas had an inventory[26] made before he sailed for Flanders. The furnishings were sumptuous and match those listed at this time in Bess of Hardwick's great palace, Hardwick Hall in Derbyshire. She was one of Elizabeth's richest

The Renaissance doorway to the Great Hall from the courtyard at Wardour Castle.

subjects. The 39 rooms at Wardour were hung with tapestries and gilded leather, there were 'Turkey Carpetts, white Taffetye Cusshens ymbrodered, pieces of Tapestrye of the Storye of Hercules and an oystrydge egg hanging in the myddell of the Gallerye.' In the Great Chamber was one extending walnut table, one dozen square stools, one servants' food cupboard with a covering of velvet fringed with silk and gold, two crimson back chairs, 26 pictures of Popes and Emperors, one small feather bed and one pair of blankets. In total, there were 192 pictures. Most remarkable of all was the Porcelain Room[27] containing 154 pieces, basins, bottles, dishes and ewers. Porcelain came only from China at this time and was very rare and expensive. Only the royal collection had so many pieces.

Perhaps Thomas himself was also an unsung patron of architecture. The evidence comes from the Banqueting House at Ansty (formerly known as the Commandery).[28] Matthew Arundell bought the village and manor of Ansty in 1594 for £3,250 from Sir Francis Zouche. In 1596 he handed it over to his son and a 1598 document refers to the renovations carried out in those years.[29] The large building by the pond may have been part of the work, built of Chilmark stone with its large room measuring 87 feet by 26. It was probably designed by the Somerset mason-architect William Arnold who worked at Montacute. The purpose of the building is not clear – was it for recreational use, riding, bowls or tennis (it is the same dimensions as the tennis court at Hampton Court)

The Banqueting House at Ansty built for Thomas Arundell when he lived at the Manor house in the 1590s

or for banquets and functions? There are many classical details but they are not executed with confidence, suggesting that the mason did not know the styles very well. The plasterwork above the North door is made from the same moulds as Robert Eaton used at Montacute and must have been done or supervised by him – pomegranates, seed pods and oak leaves.

Recently discovered plasterwork in the Banqueting House at Ansty by Robert Eaton who used the same moulds at Montacute in the 1590s.

Elizabeth died on 24 March 1603 and all Catholics had high hopes of the new King, James Stuart, King of Scotland. Thomas was granted a general pardon on 17 November 1603 under the Great Seal of the new King and on 4 May 1605 he was created Baron Arundell of Wardour, a long overdue recognition of the family's importance. Soon after, he was appointed Colonel of the English regiment for service in Flanders. This regiment was the extraordinary result of the peace treaty signed by James with the King of Spain in August 1604. In the late 16th century many English soldiers had gone to the Netherlands to fight either for the Dutch rebels against Spain or for Spain against the rebels. Elizabeth promised help to the rebels but she was half-hearted because she disapproved of rebels *per se*. A clause in the peace treaty said that Spain could recruit mercenaries in England to fight the rebels and in January 1605 the Spanish ambassador opened a recruiting office in London. Large numbers of Catholics took a temporary oath of allegiance to the King of Spain and Cecil chose someone he could trust as the colonel in charge – Thomas Arundell. He was in high favour at this time because of his loyalty to the new king[30] and his promotion of a voyage of exploration to Maine in which many courtiers had shares.

One problem was how to cross the channel without encountering the Dutch who aimed to sink all suspicious boats. In September 1605 Thomas left England in disguise, with a false beard and ragged clothing, travelling in one of the official Royal Navy ships that escorted the retiring Spanish ambassador on his way home. Thomas was stationed in Brussels with his force of 1500 soldiers. There was no military glory this time. The Spanish commander had just finished a successful campaigning season and was returning home. Officers deserted, men were not paid and a mutiny broke out in April 1606. The regiment was dissolved.

Whatever frustration Thomas may have felt, this period of service overseas had the great advantage of removing him from all involvement in the events of the Gunpowder Plot in November 1605. If he had been in England he would have been under great suspicion. As things stood, Sir William Waad, the lieutenant of the Tower and fierce enemy of recusants, sent Cecil this message on 8 November:

> Fawkes is in a most stubborn and perverse humour, as dogged as if possessed, he promised to give a full account of the Plot but now refuses. Lord Arundell, Sir Griffin Markham and one Tresham, long a pensioner of the King of Spain, are suspicious persons.[31]

Suspicious maybe, but in this case distance lent security.

Thomas lived for another 33 years after his return from the Netherlands. His beloved wife[32] died in June 1607 and he married again in 1608.[33] There were seven more children. He spent much time in London serving the King at Court and in Parliament. He was lucky that he died just a few years before the destruction of his family home at Wardour in the Civil War.[34] His life had been eventful enough.

3

To be a Catholic

IT is difficult to be precise about exactly when the Arundells, a Catholic family in Catholic England, became a Catholic family in Protestant England. There are many grey areas. Thomas the Founder probably believed that the religious turmoil he lived through was only a temporary turbulence in the steady progress of the Church. There had been such periods in the past. But when his grandson's London house was searched for 'Catholic papers' by Robert Cecil's agents in the 1590s[1] and he was thrown into prison without any exact charge, the Arundells must have realised that they belonged to a persecuted minority.

Sadly, religious beliefs are often contentious and people sometimes want their ancestors to be depicted as rigidly orthodox when such was not the case.

A good example of this is the effort made by the 12th Lord in the 1890s to excuse or conceal the acquisition of land from Shaftesbury Abbey by his ancestor in the 1540s.[2] The 12th Lord advised that the deed from his family archives which showed the purchase of monastic land from King Henry VIII should no longer be displayed in Shaftesbury Museum. He was embarrassed by it. If it had to remain on display a note should go with it to explain that Thomas the Founder had bought the land because he already owned some land in the district (hardly a good excuse) and he wanted to keep it safe, in good Catholic hands, until events settled down. But that is misreading history. Thomas Arundell bought the Shaftesbury

Abbey estates because he had money to invest and he supported the King in what appeared to be a worthwhile reform of the Church. The abbeys were fabulously wealthy. Thomas approved the King's plan to remove from thousands of monks and nuns the impediments to a good, holy life, namely the distraction of great wealth. Blessed are the poor. Acquiring land from the Church was an economic, not a theological transaction. For all Thomas knew, England would continue as a Catholic country for ever; quarrels between Kings and Popes had occurred before and eventually the rifts had been healed. So it would be again.

But in the reign of Henry's daughter Elizabeth, things were very different. Elizabeth refused to be reconciled with the Pope and began the establishment of a permanently separate Protestant national church. She began the process of enacting Penal Laws against the Catholics and other dissenters from the national Church. No one in 1559 knew she would rule for nearly 45 years. If her reign had been as short as that of her half sister, Mary, there would have been a very different outcome. Instead of a Protestant national church there might have been nothing more troublesome than a group of Protestant reformers in the north west part of Catholic Europe. There would have been no need for Thomas the Valiant and his family to begin the long years of suffering for their beliefs.

It is very unusual for any society to feel confident and secure enough to be able to live easily with difference in its midst; whether the difference arises from religious beliefs or culture or language or custom. A weak society always turns on those who are different when it feels itself threatened. In the case of religious beliefs in the 16th century, the differences were not insignificant but major. The Catholics and the reformers disagreed about how to ensure the salvation of the soul. Nothing was more important; how to prepare adequately for eternity. In our secular age we easily forget that for most of history this has been the major preoccupation of most people. And the concept that toleration might be preferable to conflict was not considered tenable. It was thought impossible for a state to tolerate religious differences in its midst because errors harmed the individuals who strayed into them and the whole of society. They must be removed by persuasion or persecution. For a Catholic to slide into a comfortable accommodation with Protestant beliefs was not possible. And vice versa. At stake was the salvation of an individual soul and nothing mattered more.

Another sure recipe for the persecution of a minority which is different, is for the majority to believe that the minority is linked with or even helping outsiders who threaten the security of the state. The result is paranoia and persecution. There is no hope that a tolerant, peaceful society might be created when disloyalty is suspected. Recently, many English people have felt uncomfortable with Muslims in their midst. A few people have chosen to believe a grotesque caricature of the Islamic faith; perhaps surprising in people who once ruled the largest Muslim empire the world has ever known, as part of the vast British Empire in Asia. Xenophobia has strange parents. But only after various mullahs' pronouncements against the West and the horror of 9/11 was Islamophobia fed by issues of national security. So it was in Elizabethan England with Catholics and their place in society.

On 22 February 1570, Pope Pius V issued his Bull *Regnans in Excelsis*.[3] He excommunicated Elizabeth, deprived her of her 'pretended title' and absolved all her subjects, even those who had sworn oaths to her, from the duty of obedience. It was dynamite. Even worse followed when it became known that the Pope was in negotiations with France and Spain to launch a joint invasion of England.[4] The Pope's political judgment was abysmal and his Bull did great harm to the Catholic cause, making it easy for every prejudiced and bigoted Protestant to support persecution. Ever afterwards, it was easy for sadistic and intolerant officials to quote 'national security' as an excuse for a fresh round of persecution of Catholics, 'who could not be trusted'. The Bull made it possible to win the support of moderate people for the persecution of Catholics. As always, such persecution only served to strengthen the resolve of the persecuted and to create martyrs who were an inspiration to their followers. The 1605 Gunpowder Plot, whatever the truth about its origins, simply made matters much worse as it provided so-called proof of the disloyalty and support for terrorism of some Catholics. The Papal Bull and the 5/11 Plot cast long shadows. It was impossible for the Catholics to shake off the suspicion that some of them might one day help England's enemies, whoever they might be.

From the reign of Elizabeth until the 18th century a series of laws, known collectively as the Penal Laws was passed against Catholics' freedom as citizens. They began with punishments for not attending the national Protestant Church, as established by Elizabeth in the 1560s and ended with the imposition of double land tax for any Catholic landowner in the 1790s. These long years of persecution are all part of our national story but seldom remembered today. It is disingenuous to claim that the Penal Laws were only a sword of Damocles hanging over the Catholic community and were seldom used. Swords should not hang over any citizens in a civilised society. The fact that the Laws existed at all is a tragedy. They deprived the whole of English society of the invaluable contribution to national life of a vigorous minority. These are some of the Penal Laws which faced a Catholic family in say, 1720: any Catholic priest could be accused of high treason and imprisoned and executed; anyone found saying or hearing Mass was liable for punishment; if any Catholic family educated children at home they paid fines and any children educated abroad could be disinherited; anyone refusing to take the Oath of Allegiance was barred from public office, the Army, the law and medicine; no baptism, marriage or burial could take place except in the Church of England;[5] there was no vote for any Catholic; a Catholic landowner must pay double land tax and register his estates, on inheritance, with the magistrates. This was England's green and pleasant land; for 250 years the home of thousands of brave Catholics who mostly withstood this persecution and suffered quietly.

Each generation of Arundells fared differently under the Penal Laws. We know that Thomas the 1st Lord decided to take the Oath of

Allegiance that James I introduced in 1606:

> I . . . do truly and sincerely acknowledge that our Sovereign lord
> King James, is lawful and rightful King and that the Pope neither
> of himself nor by any authority of Church or See of Rome has any
> power or authority to depose the King . . . I will bear faithful and
> true allegiance to his Majesty . . . and I do further swear that I do
> from my heart abhor, detest and abjure as impious and heretical this
> damnable doctrine that princes which be excommunicated by the
> Pope may be deposed or murdered by their subjects.

Thomas went on to give many years service in Parliament to King
James I and to Charles I but most Catholics found it impossible to swear
that the Pope's deposing power was heretical. A different form of words
would have been more helpful. Thomas's grandson Henry endured five
years in the Tower and almost lost his life in the 1680s for his Catholic
beliefs. All through the 18th century the Arundells were barred from
public service, went abroad to St. Omers in France to be educated and
paid double land tax.

It is a pointless exercise to collect examples of where local,
friendly magistrates turned a blind eye to contraventions of the Penal
Laws or where they were held permanently in abeyance. The fact that
they existed was enough to blight the lives of thousands of English
people. And violence sometimes broke out. The Gordon Riots erupted
in London in June 1780 when Lord George Gordon presented a petition
to Parliament against granting any concessions to Catholics. The mob
went on the rampage, destroyed Catholic chapels, burnt Catholic houses
and attacked Catholic families. By the end, there were 700 dead in
London. The 8th Lord was at Wardour and feared that a mob would
destroy the new chapel. He had to send to Salisbury for a detachment
of soldiers to guard it. The Catholic chapel was destroyed in Bath and
many Catholics there lost their homes and belongings.

PIVS VI.   PONT. MAX.
Equitans in Possessionem   *Banlicæ Lateranensis*

An unusual picture of Pope Pius VI (1775-1799) on horseback, sent to the 8th Lord as a souvenir from Rome. It is the only known picture of a Pope on horseback.

Henry the 8th Lord was heavily involved in the moves towards Catholic emancipation in the late 18th century.[6] A great leader of the campaign was the politician, Charles James Fox. It may be the reason why Fox's gold pocket watch became a treasured Arundell family heirloom.[7] Fox spoke out many times in favour of equal rights for Catholics. He said in the House of Commons on 19 April 1791, 'toleration in religion is one of the great rights of man and a man ought never to be deprived of what is his natural right.' But the fight for freedom for Catholics was not a straightforward campaign. There were many disagreements about how it should be fought. Boxes of papers in the family archives are testimony to Lord Arundell's views and arguments. He did not support his friend Lord Petre's Catholic Committee, which wanted to negotiate with the government and offer concessions. They proposed to accept an oath that was 'schismatical, scandalous, inflammatory and insulting to the Supreme Head of the Church, the Pope' (in the words of the Catholic Vicars Apostolic who produced an Evangelical Letter against it).[8] Arundell believed that freedom should come as a right and not as a concession based on negotiation. But progress was made in June 1778 with a small Relief Act which lifted the penalties on priests and provided a new Oath of Allegiance. The Gordon Riots were the result.

The next stage was the much larger Relief Act of 1791, repealing the recusancy laws, allowing the building of Catholic chapels and schools and abolishing double land tax. But still there was the ban on holding public office, on voting and on burials in Catholic cemeteries. (The last Arundell who had to be buried in Tisbury Anglican Church was the 9th Lord in July 1817).[9] In 1829 came the Emancipation Act, 270 years after the persecution had started. The Test and Corporation Acts were abolished and all other restrictions removed so Catholics could at last play a full part in public life. Free at last!

Thereafter the Catholic community at Wardour flourished as never before. There had always been Catholic priests at Wardour; in the old castle where recusants' graffiti bears witness to the struggle for survival; in Old Wardour House where a chapel was built against the South bailey wall and in the new Castle where a suite of rooms beside the magnificent chapel was set aside for the priests. The Catholic community at Wardour was long thought to be the largest Catholic community outside London, served by Jesuit priests from the late 16th century until 2003 in almost unbroken line. The Arundells set up and supported chapels in Ansty and Donhead and gave generous donations towards the building of the Church of the Sacred Heart in Tisbury.[10] On Sunday, 25 March 1851 a census was held throughout the country to count the number of people attending churches on that day. The three services in Wardour chapel were attended by a total of 830 people which was said to be a smaller number than usual. The total attendance in the Catholic churches in Salisbury was only 145.[11] The Wardour figures must have been a source of pride for the Arundell family.

Graffiti on a wall at the old castle, believed to show that the nearby room was used as a Catholic chapel during Penal times.

The chapel in the new castle consecrated on All Saints' Day, 1 November 1776 by Bishop Walmesley.

4

Maryland

A FAMILY may acquire many honours over the centuries – titles, medals, positions of power, but one of the greatest honours a family can claim is that they founded a state in America and laid down principles for its government that advanced human freedom and happiness. This is the story of the Arundells and the state of Maryland.

When Thomas Arundell was in disgrace with Elizabeth in the 1590s, he often proposed that he would equip and lead a voyage of discovery to new lands across the seas and thereby redeem himself.[1] His plans came to nothing but one of his friends, George Calvert, had spectacular success with similar ambitions. Calvert's son Cecil married Arundell's daughter Anne and thus the families were linked by more than friendship.

George Calvert was born in Yorkshire to a Catholic family in 1580.[2] They conformed to the state church on the surface but retained their Catholic convictions, probably in the same way as the Arundells. George was a brilliant linguist and a lawyer. In 1603 he entered Robert Cecil's service as one

Cecil Calvert, 2nd Lord Baltimore who married Anne Arundell and lived with her at Hook Manor, Donhead, then known as Baltimore House.

Anne Arundell, the 1st Lord's seventh child who married Cecil Calvert in 1628 and helped him to found Maryland.

of his secretaries and rose to become Clerk of the Privy Council. The King, James I, made him Secretary of State in 1619 and he was put in charge of the negotiations with Spain for the marriage of Prince Charles, the Prince of Wales, to the Infanta. All this time his eyes were on distant horizons and he invested his earnings in the East India Company, the Virginia Company and in buying land in Newfoundland, land which was hardly explored by Europeans By 1623 the royal marriage negotiations were deadlocked and Calvert decided to resign as Secretary of State and announce openly his loyalty to the Catholic Church. The King retained him as a councillor and made him Lord Baltimore, so named after a place near his estate in southern Ireland. Unfortunately, his government service came to an end in 1625 when he refused to take the Oath of Allegiance.[3] His attention then turned to North America. He had obtained a charter for a province to be called Avalon[4] in Newfoundland in 1623 and in 1627 he visited it with his family. The visit was not a success; cold, disease and French attacks had decimated the settlers so Calvert decided to abandon the site and sail for Virginia. In 1630 he petitioned the King for a grant of land along Chesapeake Bay and in June 1632, a few weeks after he died in London, the Maryland Charter received the Great Seal. The settlement was named after the new King's wife, Henrietta Maria. The Calverts thus became proprietors of seven million acres and hereditary rulers of

Maryland, with absolute powers, which continued until the Declaration of Independence in 1776.

Lord Baltimore's eldest son, Cecil was only 28 when his father died and he inherited the settlement in North America. He was named Cecil after Robert Cecil who was also his godfather, when he was baptised in 1606 in the Anglican Church. Despite this, he was brought up as a Catholic and on a visit to Rome in 1623 he publicly announced his loyalty to the Catholic faith. He married in 1628 Anne Arundell,[5] Thomas's

third daughter and a house, now named Hook Manor, near Wardour Castle, came to them as Anne's marriage gift.[6] This is the place where their five children were born and where many of the plans for the new colony were made.

Cecil Calvert decided to stay in England and send his brother Leonard as Governor of the new colony. A ceiling of a room in the east wing of Hook Manor still reminds us

A 17th century ship depicted in plasterwork on a ceiling in Hook Manor and believed to represent the Ark or the Dove, which took settlers to Maryland.

The initials of Anne Arundell and Cecil Calvert on the drawing room ceiling at Hook Manor.

of those days, with its depiction of the *Ark* and the *Dove*, the two ships that sailed to the new colony in November 1633 with 140 Catholic and Protestant settlers. They arrived in Chesapeake Bay in late February 1634 and celebrated Mass in thanksgiving. The monograms CC and AA, for Cecil Calvert and Anne Arundell, are also depicted on the plasterwork of the ceiling amidst the dolphins, roses, whales and fleurs-de-lis.[7] Cecil ruled Maryland for 43 years, initially from this house, taking the title of Proprietor of Maryland.

What plans did they make for the new settlement? First, that it should make a good profit, especially from the trade in beaver fur; the family had lost £25,000 in the Avalon adventure. Secondly, that it should help Catholics who wanted to start a new life in peace and prosperity and thirdly, underpinning all the rest, that it should be a place where freedom of conscience was practised, a new model for Church–state relations. This last aspect was revolutionary.[8] Throughout Europe it was accepted that subjects should follow the religion of their ruler and that uniformity must be enforced for the sake of salvation and peace. But Catholic survival and service to Elizabeth, through years of persecution, had been a validation of the different attitude that religion should be a private matter. Cecil's father had demonstrated in his career that loyalty to his faith and loyalty to his country were not incompatible. Anne's father had walked the fine line of service to the King while retaining his faith. Despite all that, how easy it would have been to attempt to organise the new colony on the basis that Catholics should be protected and given privileged positions, simply because they were Catholics. Cecil and Anne rejected that as also they rejected a simple reproduction of the status quo in England with its Oath of Allegiance and penalties against dissenters.

It is good to think of the young couple making their plans in Hook Manor at Wardour and on 13 November 1633, perhaps in the room with the decorated ceiling, Cecil drew up a List of Instructions. He put the burden of restraint on the Catholics in the colony: 'all Acts of Romane Catholique Religion to be done as privately as may be and all Romane Catholics to be silent upon all occasions of discourse concerning matters of Religion.' There was to be no religious qualification for holding office;

the Jesuits were not to be given any special privileges although they requested them. Government officers were not to trouble or molest any persons professing to believe in Jesus Christ, so long as they remained loyal and obedient to the proprietor.

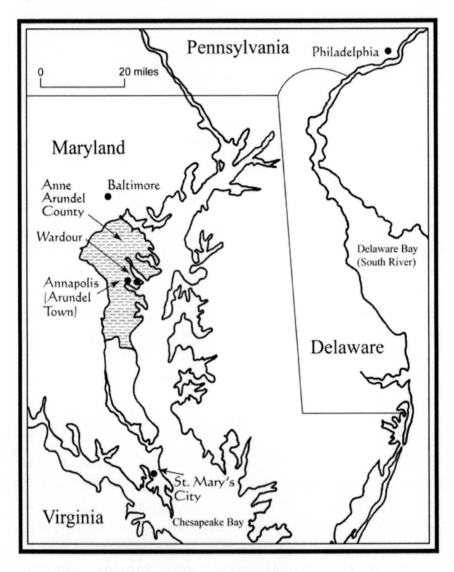

Places in the American state of Maryland connected with Anne Arundell's family.

Inevitably it was not all plain sailing. Conflicts arose. In July 1638 Capt. Lewis, a Catholic officer, was fined the huge amount of 500 lb of tobacco because he had forbidden servants from reading books of Puritan sermons. He was told it was none of his business to interfere with what people read.[9] Spiritual loyalty and temporal loyalty were quite separate. Religion was a private matter.

In 1649 the Assembly passed an Act Concerning Religion, drafted by Baltimore and summing up all the principles which he and his wife held dear. The aim was to demonstrate that more than one expression of Christian belief was possible under the same government. The use of derogatory religious terms was outlawed. Marylanders could no longer call a fellow citizen,

an Heretick, Schismatick,[10] Idolater, Puritan, Presbyterian, Antinomian,[11] Barrowist,[12] Separatist, Popish priest, Jesuit, Papist, Lutheran, Calvinist, Anabaptist, Brownist,[13] or any other name in an insulting manner. There are penalties for anyone who profanes the Sabbath by swearing, drunkenness or disorderly recreation. No one who professes to believe in Jesus Christ shall be any ways troubled, molested or discountenanced for or in respect of his or her Religion nor in the free exercise thereof within this Province. No Christian shall be compelled to the belief or exercise of any other Religion against his or her consent simply to demonstrate loyalty to the proprietor.

This was the first law in the English-speaking world that guaranteed toleration to all Christians. Although there were later in the century many problems in Maryland with regard to the power of the Governor and the beliefs of the inhabitants, the founders had won for themselves a great place in the history of religious liberty. Sadly Anne Calvert died in 1649 at Wardour when she was only 33. She is buried in the chancel of Tisbury Church. Around the edge of her tombstone are

Anne Calvert's tomb in the chancel of Tisbury church, describing her as
"most beautiful and most noble." She died in 1649.

these words in Latin: 'Anne Arundell, the most beautiful and best wife
of Cecil Calvert, Lord Baltimore and absolute lord of Maryland and
Avalon, and most beloved daughter of the 1st Lord Arundell of Wardour,
Count of the Holy Roman Empire.'[14] It would perhaps be appropriate to
place flowers on her grave every anniversary of her death on 10th June,
in memory of all those who have fought for religious freedom and still
have to fight today.

5

Lady Blanche and the Civil War

EVERY war is a tragedy and none more than a civil war. Families, villages and towns are torn apart by conflicting loyalties. Wars all arise from the failure of politicians to use their negotiating skills effectively. In the 1630s King Charles was convinced that his enemies in Parliament were plotting to kill him and his family. Parliamentary leaders were convinced that the King was plotting with the Pope to destroy the Protestant religion. There was a complete breakdown of trust. The King's nerve broke first and on 22 August 1642, he raised his standard at Nottingham. Fighting took the place of talking. But war could have been averted if the leaders had shown more skill.

The Civil War was, like all others, a brutal war, involving perhaps a quarter of the population in fighting at one time or another.[1] Hunger, cold and disease are the normal companions of war and the terrible injuries that befall those directly involved. A musket shot was lethal at 50 yards or less. It made an entry wound half an inch across and an exit wound the size of a dinner plate. How much a community suffered in the 1640s depended on the involvement of its landowner in the war, its position on the route of marching armies and its proximity to a siege.

As usual, the names of most ordinary men and women are missing from the records. The villagers of Ansty, Wardour and Tisbury must have been heavily involved in the fighting at Wardour Castle but we do not know how many died or how many families were torn apart.

William Waller, a Parliamentary leader wrote from Bath to his friend Ralph Hopton, the Royalist, in Wells, on 16 June 1643. He bewailed their involvement in 'this war without an Enemie' and continued: 'Wee are both upon the stage and must act those parts that are assigned to us in this Tragedy. Lett us do it in a way of honour and without personal animosities, whatsoever the issue may be.'[2]

Wiltshire was a rich, farming county with about 110,000 people, strategically important on the route to the West. By the end of 1642, the county was almost all under Parliamentary control. 21 out of the 29 MPs supported Parliament, the militia was under its control and Salisbury, Chippenham, Marlborough and Devizes had all opted for Parliament. Lord Pembroke was appointed Parliament's Lord Lieutenant with orders to raise extra money and horse. The rebel commanders were Sir Edward Hungerford and Sir Edward Baynton. They quarrelled bitterly in the winter of 1642 and arrested each other but eventually Hungerford was appointed sole commander.

The Arundells in the south west were exceptions to the general support for Parliament. They had sworn undying loyalty to the King, given him £500 in 1639 and raised a troop of horse for his service. The 2nd Lord was away in Oxford with the King, leaving his wife Lady Blanche in charge of the castle at Wardour. She heard the news in October 1642 that the Battle of Edgehill was indecisive and that the King had

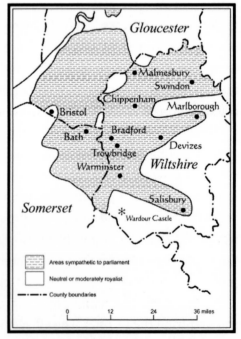

Map to show the loyalties of Wiltshire people during the Civil War, 1642-1646.

Lady Blanche, heroine of the siege of Wardour as she would not have looked during military operations, painted by Angelica Kauffman in the 1770s.

issued a proclamation of 'grace, favour and pardon' to all inhabitants of Wiltshire except the four traitors (Sir Edward Hungerford, Sir Henry Ludlow, Sir John Evelyn and Walter Long) who were leaders of the Parliamentary forces.

But perhaps things were turning in the King's favour because on 5 December 1642, Royalist soldiers captured Marlborough, the first garrison town in England to change hands. More royalist success followed when Prince Rupert occupied Malmesbury for the King in February 1643 and the King's forces then took Devizes. Parliament countered with an order for the confiscation of all Royalist estates. In April, Hungerford plundered Longleat[3] and then moved on to begin the siege of Wardour Castle, at the centre of the richest Royalist estate in the south of the county.

The contemporary evidence for the story of the first siege of Wardour is limited to the account published in *Mercurius Rusticus* on 17 June 1643.[4] This was a short-lived Royalist newssheet edited by Bruno Ryves, one of the King's chaplains and printed in Oxford. Truth is the first casualty of war and it is therefore not surprising that the subtitle of the newssheet was *The Countries Complaint of the Murthers, Robberies, Plunderings and other outrages committed by the Rebells on His Majesties faithful Subjects.* The aim of the editor was to present to the public vivid accounts of atrocities allegedly committed by the Parliamentary armies. Nothing pleased him more than a good story involving a brave woman, her daughter-in-law and grandchildren holding out against a cruel enemy. Fortitude displayed by a garrison was evidence of divine favour. It is thus extremely difficult to know exactly what happened at Wardour Castle in May 1643, with any regard to the truth.

There is, however, another account of the siege published in *The Catholic Magazine* in 1838. At the time this was believed to be a long-lost account written by Lady Blanche herself and 'discovered in the archives'. The story is full of high drama. Cannon balls crash into the castle walls, Mass in the chapel is interrupted only momentarily when

Marble effigy of Sir Edward Hungerford on his tomb in the chapel of Farleigh Hungerford Castle. He besieged Wardour Castle in 1643 and forced Lady Blanche to surrender.

a cannon ball lodges in the wall above the altar, matchlocks protrude from every window and spread terror among the assailants, lead is torn from the roof to provide bullets . . . and through it all, Lady Arundell remains strong and steadfast. 'I know no Parliamentary army; troops of rebels are there in the field, enemies alike to their royal master and to his loyal subjects. I will treat with none of these.' Unfortunately this is a fictitious account written by the Dowager Lady Arundell, widow of the 10th Lord, in the 1830s. She was apparently greatly amused when people were taken in by it. History may be only someone's story but this is not history.[5]

Back to *Mercurius Rusticus*. The siege began on Tuesday 2 May 1643. Hungerford soon realised that the occupants of the castle would not surrender without a struggle. He therefore called on Colonel

Strode to bring reinforcements and there were eventually 1300 men surrounding the small garrison of 25 servants led by Lady Arundell[6] with her daughter-in-law Cicely, her two grandsons Thomas and Henry and granddaughter Cicely. None of Lady Arundell's men had any military training. Hungerford ordered a trumpeter to give the signal for surrender but Lady Arundell refused to consider it, saying that she would only surrender the castle to her husband who had told her to keep it for him.

On Wednesday 3 May, the enemy placed cannons 'within Musket shot', on the hillsides surrounding the castle and began the bombardment which lasted until the following Monday.[7] Mines were placed in the vaults beneath the castle and some caused great damage when they exploded. The modern drains installed in the 1580s made the castle very vulnerable. The rebels then offered to give quarter[8] or clemency to the women and children but not to the men. This was refused by Lady Arundell.

Hunger and exhaustion began to weaken the garrison, so much so that 'when they have endeavoured to administer food, surprised with sleep, it (their arm) forgot its employment, the morsels falling from their hands while they were about to eat, deluding their appetites.' The maid servants bravely loaded the muskets for the men to keep them fighting.[9] The enemy brought up small cannons to attack the garden doors and threw burning missiles into the broken windows. In all, the rebels lost at least 60 men, killed by musket shot but the defenders lost only one. It seems extraordinary that the castle, which was really no more than a fortified manor house, took so long to capture. Was the truth perhaps different from this exaggerated account which the Royalists wanted to present to the world?

After five days, Lady Arundell decided to order a parley to be sounded,[10] so desperate was the situation. But she demanded and surprisingly obtained good terms: that everyone in the castle should have quarter; that women and servants should take away with them

Lady Arundell directing the defence of Wardour Castle as imagined by a Victorian artist in Cattermole's History. This version is by Anton Bantock.

all their clothes and the women should have six men with them as servants; that all the furniture and goods in the castle should be safe from plunder and listed in an inventory to be made by one of the servants. However, the rebels could not be trusted and broke their word. The women took away only the clothes they were wearing and their trunks were seized. The contents of the castle were ransacked; a chimney piece worth £2000[11] was destroyed and all the pictures, 'a loss that neither Cost nor Art can repair', in the words of the report in *Mercurius Rusticus*.

Lady Arundell and her family were taken to Shaftesbury as prisoners. The work of destruction continued in the park – killing the deer, cutting down the trees, emptying the ponds of fish and even digging up the lead water pipe that supplied the castle and selling it for six pence a yard. It was 'as if the present generation were too narrow an object for their rage and they plundered posterity.' Total losses were over £100,000.

Even worse things befell the family. The rebels decided to send them all to Bath where an epidemic of smallpox and plague was raging. Despite being ill, old Lady Arundell refused to move. The rebels realised that they would do their cause only harm by such cruelty to the family. They therefore decided to send the two young boys (one nine and the other seven) on their own to Dorchester, a town infected with 'Schisme and Rebellion.'[12] The mother's tears and pleas fell on deaf ears.

For this barbarity, the newssheet considered, it would be necessary to go outside Christendom to find a precedent amongst 'unwashed Turks who take Christian children from their Mothers breasts either to make them Janissary guards or Eunuchs for their concubines.' If the purpose of removing the boys was to educate them in the 'true religion' then this also was against the laws of God and man. The writer then admits that 'a just indignation against so barbarous a practice hath transported me in this argument farther than I intended, though not so far as the heinousness of the fact deserves . . .'

Such was the material for a Royalist legend and the final ingredient was the news that reached Lady Arundell later in Salisbury that her husband had been mortally wounded at the Battle of Stratton on 16 May and died in Oxford a few days later.

This magnificent Great Hall fireplace was destroyed by Hungerford's men in 1643. It was said to be worth more than £2,000; reconstructed in this drawing by Peter Dunn.

But it is worth comparing some of the details of post–surrender treatment in the newssheet, with the surrender agreement signed by

Hungerford and Strode and accepted by Lady Arundell on 8 May 1643.[13] The document is still in the family archives. Both versions agree that all defenders should have quarter; both agree that respect should be shown to the gentlewomen and that they should take all their clothes with them. But they diverge in several ways. Hungerford promised that the gentlewomen and their servants should be conveyed to Bath 'if her Ladyship like not of Bristoll' (so why did she protest about going to Bath when that was part of the surrender agreement?); Hungerford stated that the castle and all its contents were to be surrendered and an inventory made 'untill the further pleasure of the Parliament bee signified therein' (no mention of furniture and goods being safe from confiscation or that they were to be listed in an inventory to prevent this). The separation of children from their mother was not mentioned at all so it may have arisen out of negotiations in Shaftesbury. Subtle differences maybe, but in such ways is propaganda fed and truth suffers.

Meanwhile, the Royalist forces in the rest of Wiltshire were gaining ground. In July 1643, Prince Rupert captured Malmesbury and the Royalist army celebrated a great victory at Roundway Down near Devizes. Chippenham and Devizes were besieged by Royalist troops.

At Wardour, Colonel Edmund Ludlow, who had arrived on 8 May, was made Governor. Although the castle had suffered considerable damage it was still defendable. Ludlow was a captain of a troop of horse in Hungerford's regiment, born in Maiden Bradley in 1617. His father, a Wiltshire MP, was an outspoken

Captain Edmund Ludlow, appointed governor of Wardour Castle from May 1643 to March 1644, was responsible for the looting of the contents.

critic of the King. He believed that Parliament's cause was God's cause. Ludlow was later one of the King's judges at his trial in January 1649 and his was the 40th signature on the death warrant that led to the King's execution on 30 January 1649. In 1660 he went into exile in Switzerland and wrote his memoirs called *A Voyce from the Watch Tower*. They were published in 1698, six years after his death. Looking back, he explained quite simply what the war had been about:

> The question in dispute between the King's party and us being, as I apprehended, whether the King should govern as a god by his will and the nation be governed by force like beasts; or whether the people should be governed by laws made by themselves and live under a government derived from their own consent.

Ludlow's memoirs provide our main source for the recapture of the castle. They are as unreliable as anyone's memoirs.

The second siege of Wardour Castle began in June 1643. Ludlow had scarcely time to sink a well, break down the remaining vaults and fill the castle with provisions before the new Lord Arundell, the 2nd Lord's only son Henry, arrived 'within a fortnight'. He demanded surrender but Ludlow refused saying, 'I was entrusted to keep the castle for the service of the Parliament and cannot surrender it without their command.' The enemy then withdrew and, perversely, gave the defenders time to buy more supplies and ammunition from Southampton. Money was in short supply so they were very lucky to find gold and jewels worth £1200 walled up in the castle. The enemy began to draw closer again and it was decided to fire the harquebus[14] from the roof of the castle but it burst in the middle and exploded. The cause was a mystery until it was linked with a twelve year old boy who, a few days previously, had been taken on as a spit-turner in the kitchens. He aroused the suspicion of the guards and they eventually forced him to confess that he had been sent in as a spy to count the number of defenders, immobilise the guns and poison the wells and the beer. Weeks of waiting and watching followed. The autumn and early winter days were quiet.

In December 1643 the besiegers collected reinforcements and positioned themselves behind an earthwork facing the main gate. Shots were exchanged and the Royalist commander Capt. Bowyer was wounded in the heel. He died soon after from gangrene. The new Royalist commander was Col. Barnes whose brother was the Ludlows' family chaplain. He built a fort on the hillside behind the castle, 'within musket-shot of us.'

Various sorties were made out of the castle, a few prisoners were taken and one of the defenders was killed. The King sent a relative of Ludlow to offer terms. Ludlow invited him into the castle and so arranged the barrels and boxes of food that it looked as if there was plenty. Ludlow agreed to surrender only if there was no relief within six months, the castle should no longer be used as a garrison and £2000 compensation should be paid to Parliament for its expenditure. The terms were not accepted. In truth, supplies were very low. 'Our beer was now spent, our corn much diminished and we had no drink but the water of our well which, though we drink it dry every day, yet it was sufficiently supplied every night.' The garrison of nearly 100 men had to survive on reduced rations which were 'so short that I caused one of the horses we had taken to be killed, which the soldiers ate up in two days besides their ordinary.'

But the defenders' spirits rose when one of Ludlow's men escaped from the castle and met an enemy soldier who promised to help them by wearing a white cap and blowing his nose with a handkerchief when relief was coming! The besiegers then damaged the portcullis by a shot which cut the chain so a window had to be used as a door. The enemy began mining under the castle walls to place gunpowder or light a fire but they were driven off by boiling water and molten lead dropped on them from the roof and hand grenades thrown at them.

At this point, Sir Ralph Hopton the Royalist commander in the West sent Sir Francis Doddington[15] to organise the capture of the castle, with an engineer and the 'miners of Mendip to assist them'. Ludlow later remembered that they could hear the noise of their digging every night. Doddington sent a letter advising Ludlow to surrender, adding that he would grant him any favour. Ludlow replied that he would cheerfully lay down his life 'in defence of the laws and liberties of the nation'. He was perhaps aware that Wardour Castle was the last Parliamentary garrison in Wiltshire and if it fell, Wiltshire would be entirely in Royalist hands.

The next development is best told in Ludlow's own words:

The two nights following we all continued upon the guard; and upon the Thursday morning, being very weary, I lay down and slept till between ten or eleven of the clock, at which time one of my great guns firing upon the enemy, shook the match which they had left burning for the springing of the mine, so that the mine springing I was lifted up with it from the floor, with much dust suddenly about me; which was no sooner laid but I found both the doors of my chamber blown open and my window towards the enemy blown down, so that a cart might have entered at the breach.

The party which they had prepared to storm us lay at some distance, to secure themselves from any hurt by the springing of the mine; but that being done they made haste to storm, which they might easily do at my window, the rubbish of the Castle having made them a way almost to it. My pistols being wheel-locks and wound up all night I could not get to fire;[16] so that I was forced to trust to my sword for the keeping down of the enemy, being alone in the chamber, and all relief excluded from me except such as came in by one of my windows that looked into the court of the castle; through which I called to my men there, acquainting them with my condition and requiring them to hasten to my relief.

Many rooms were similarly damaged and Ludlow tried to organise men to defend them. The enemy asked permission to carry

The destruction by an explosion of the south west side of the castle on 14 March 1644, as imagined by Anton Bantock.

away wounded men from the ground and this was granted but when Ludlow asked the same it was refused and one of his men died a slow, agonising death over three days. Surprisingly only three men were lost in the explosion but all the corn was destroyed. Mr Balsum the minister then came to Ludlow with a request that he should propose a treaty with the enemy, telling him, 'all the blood that should be spilt in further opposition would be charged upon my account'. A parley with the enemy was called but Lord Arundell refused, despite having lost ten men himself and many of his soldiers wounded in the attack.

One of the Royalist dead was Hillsdeane,

who a little before he expired said he saw his brother fire that musket by which he received his mortal wound: which might probably be;

his brother being one of those who defended that breach where he, attempting to enter, was shot.

Then suddenly, the Royalists proposed a truce. Ludlow agreed to surrender on suitable terms but negotiations dragged on and were eventually abandoned. 'And now the spirits of my soldiers began to flag.' They begged Ludlow to surrender. Ludlow realised the desperate situation:

> having ten doors blown open by the first mine, our walls that stood being cracked in several places and another mine ready to spring, that would probably level the most part of the castle with the ground and not having provision sufficient for one day left, nor any hopes of relief.

Ludlow decided to surrender but still asked for good terms: quarter for the lives of everyone; good treatment; no one to be taken to Oxford. Lord Arundell readily agreed and Ludlow went to meet him and Sir Francis Doddington. Lord Arundell treated Ludlow extremely amicably. It was 18 March 1644 and with the surrender of the castle, the whole of Wiltshire became Royalist. 'Thus all things being agreed upon, I returned to the castle and ordered my soldiers to lay down their arms.' The men were collected in one room and put under guard but Ludlow and three friends were given the liberty of the place, upon parole. 'Their civility to me was such, especially that of Lord Arundell, that I discovered to him the plate and other things that I had hid in the castle.'

Unfortunately this amity did not last. After two days, the Royalists decided to take away two of Ludlow's men who had previously been on their side; Ludlow protested that this was against the terms of surrender, 'quarter without distinction'. The Royalists argued that the men were really theirs and should abide by their rules. Ludlow replied that God would be their judge if they behaved in such a despicable way. A meeting was held and Ludlow warned the Royalists about shedding innocent blood and that they would one day have to account for it but despite all this, two soldiers were executed and others were sent to Oxford against the terms of the surrender. Such is the sadness of war. There was no monopoly of virtue on the Royalist side.

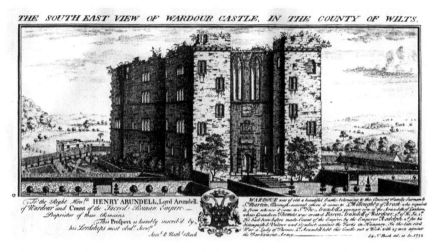

A southeast view of the castle as a ruin in 1732 by Samuel and Nathaniel Buck.

We have no means of judging the accuracy of Ludlow's memory 30 years after the events he describes. How much was exaggerated, how much dramatised? We simply do not know. The one good aspect of all this is the behaviour of Ludlow and Arundell towards each other. Ludlow was described as 'waging war like a gentleman and not like a fanatic'. Arundell later intervened with the King to save Ludlow's life and many years later Ludlow remembered this and spoke up for Arundell in Parliament against the confiscation of his estates. There is no such thing as a happy ending to a war but, as far as the Arundells were concerned, this was better than it might have been. The castle was ruined but their estates were intact and their honour was enhanced.

6

Politics, Power and Plots

IF proximity to the centre of power could be recorded on a graph for the whole Arundell family, Henry the 3rd Lord would be at the highest point alongside his great, great grandfather, Thomas the Founder. Both spent many years at Court, serving their Kings but Henry reached high office and was for nearly two years Lord Privy Seal in the reign of James II. He also lived longer than any head of the family before or since, dying in 1696 at the age of 88.

His life was the roller coaster anyone involved in 17th century politics might have expected. His father died from wounds received when he fought for the King at the battle of Stratton in 1643.[1] He himself was responsible for the destruction of Wardour Castle when he ordered it to be mined in 1644 in order to dislodge Colonel Ludlow and his men. At the end of the Civil war all his estates were confiscated by Parliament but he made an agreement that they should be looked after by trustees and they were returned to him in 1660, worth £35,000. In 1653 he took part in a duel on Putney Heath when he fought as a second to his brother-in-law, Col. Henry Compton, against Lord Chandos. Compton was killed and Chandos and Arundell were sentenced to be burnt in the hand and imprisoned for a year. Dorothy Osborne wrote: 'It was done to them both a day or two after, but very favourably. These were the first peers that had been burned in the hand.'[2] Wisely, Henry then went into exile in France and joined the royal family in Paris.

On 29 May 1660 Charles II entered London in triumph and remained King for the next 25 years. Throughout that time Henry was one of his close advisers and courtiers, although he never held any political office during the reign. That did not prevent him from suffering greatly at the time of the Titus Oates Plot in 1678, that most notorious of anti-Catholic fabrications. Henry was imprisoned in the Tower for over five years, the longest period for any member of a family which had more acquaintance with the inside of prisons than most. Within a year of his release, he was made a Privy Councillor by the new King, James II, and then in March 1687 Lord Privy Seal, a role which involved close contact with the King. When the new king fled to France in December 1688 Henry lost his place at Court and spent the rest of his life enjoying country life at Breamore[3] and Wardour, until his death in 1694.

We know very little about Henry's domestic circumstances. He married Cicely Compton in 1632 and had three children. The daughter, also Cicely, is remembered because of the picture her parents ordered for her from John Wright in 1665. She became a nun and entered the convent of the Poor Clares at Gravelines near Rouen in 1662. The nuns were forbidden to have personal possessions so the picture, for the chapel, showed Christ on the Cross with two figures (her parents) kneeling before it. The picture was sold at the time of the French Revolution and rescued and returned to Wardour.

Unfortunately no letters or account books survive from this period except a few notes in preparation for Henry's trial, which was set for January 1681 and the poems that he wrote in prison in the Tower. It is likely that he organised the building of Old Wardour House, against the bailey wall of the old castle, as a base in Wardour for the family. He is also credited with building the Banqueting House in the grounds of the old castle ruins at Wardour. It was a place to entertain friends and visitors to the ruins.

King Charles II has not been admired for any great achievements except his own survival as King, which was perhaps a greater test of

Henry 3rd Lord Arundell and his wife Cicely kneeling before Christ on the cross, painted about 1665 for the convent of English Poor Clares at Gravelines near Rouen. Their only daughter Cicely entered the convent in 1662. (The Weiss Gallery)

political skill than most contemporaries realised. He played his cards close to his chest, was a supreme performer and never let principles or friendships stand in the way of his own survival. Charles James Fox, the 18th century politician and compulsive womaniser, called him 'a disgrace to the history of our country'⁴ although on the principle that people in glasshouses don't throw stones he was obviously not referring to the King's large number of mistresses and his seventeen acknowledged bastards. The worst charge against Charles is that he allowed the hysteria of the Oates Plot in the period 1678 to 1684, to result in the execution of 35 innocent men, including 15 priests and the long imprisonment of several of his most loyal friends. The King knew that the Plot was a total fabrication and originally expressed doubts about it but he failed to reduce its fatal impact.

Henry's attachment to the new King was not just because he had lost his father, his home and his estates in service to the King's father but because the King was known to be sympathetic to the Catholic faith. The King's mother, wife and many of his mistresses were Catholics. But Charles's own feelings were well concealed. When his father sent him to join his mother in exile in Paris in 1645, the King insisted that the mother should have no control over her son's spiritual life because she was a Catholic. Charles I had suffered enough from disputes over his own religious beliefs. After his restoration in May 1660 people looked for signs that the king would make a move to the old faith but there were none. It was said of him that, 'both at prayers and at sacrament he, as it were, took care to satisfy people that he was in no sort concerned in that about which he was employed.'⁵ That was a harsh comment but Charles knew that he walked on a knife-edge and that nothing inflamed the public more than religious argument. His own attitude was to be tolerant of all religious groups, even the Quakers, and to insist that he must remain the Supreme Governor of the Church of England. Within that limitation it is perhaps surprising that Charles capitulated so frequently in the face of anti Catholic hysteria.

In December 1662 the King issued a Declaration of Indulgence and planned to remove the Penal Laws. There was an outcry in Parliament and the proposals were dropped. In September 1666 the Great Fire swept through London. The King made a visit to his suffering people and in the face of anti Catholic hysteria told them 'no plots by Frenchmen or Dutchmen or Papists have any part in bringing you so much misery.'[6] But he allowed Parliament to ban Catholic priests and enforce the Penal Laws more harshly than usual. Then, on 25 January 1669 came the most extraordinary example of Charles's machiavellian outlook. It was the Feast of the Conversion of St. Paul. Charles called a secret meeting with Arundell, Clifford, Arlington and his brother James. With tears in his eyes he said that he had decided to convert to the Catholic faith and would announce this publicly, but only when he had secretly arranged for Louis XIV of France to give him a large subsidy to accompany his conversion. Lord Arundell, under cover of his role as Master of the Horse to Queen Henrietta Maria who was living at the French Court, was sent to France to arrange the details. The Treaty, with its secret clause, was signed by Arundell and his colleagues at Dover in May 1670.[7] The main part of the Treaty pledged England and France to a joint attack on the Dutch and not to make a separate peace with them. When the King announced the treaty to Parliament and told them there were no secret clauses it was observed that his hand shook.

Rumours swept London about the King's real intentions but he felt safe enough in March 1672 to issue another Declaration of Indulgence. This suspended the Penal Laws and allowed Catholics to worship freely in private. But the opposition grew and as previously, Charles abandoned his moves towards toleration. A severe Test Act was then passed by Parliament, requiring all office holders not only to take the Oaths of Allegiance and Supremacy but to declare against basic articles of the Catholic faith. Charles was determined to die as King so he put up no resistance and let down his Catholic friends once again.

But worse was to follow. On 13 August 1678 the King was walking in St James's Park. A stranger gave him a letter. It contained details of a Catholic plot. The King was very sceptical but passed it to his advisers who began an investigation. Meanwhile, a man called Titus Oates[8] appeared before Westminster magistrates and swore on oath that all the details

Titus Oates whose 'discovery' of a fabricated Catholic plot resulted in the 3rd Lord spending five years in the Tower; engraved by R. White, 'the true Originall taken from the Life'

of the plot were true. Oates was the son of a Baptist preacher, from a violent home. He was expelled from school, ordained in the Anglican Church, expelled from his parish, then from the Navy and from the Duke of Norfolk's household. He was received into the Catholic Church in 1677 and was sent to the English Jesuit College in Spain but was expelled from there[9] and then went to the seminary at St. Omer before his final expulsion. In view of this turbulent background it is perhaps surprising that his words were taken seriously but such was the latent anti-Catholic hysteria that it needed only one spark to ignite the whole bonfire of prejudice and hatred.

Oates said the plot was master-minded by the Jesuits; they planned to depose the King and send him to a convent; five lords (Arundell, Powis, Stafford, Belayse and Petre) would rule under instructions from the Pope; Lord Arundell was to lead a military uprising, helped by 20,0000 Spanish troops and to be made Lord Chancellor. There were so many inconsistencies and contradictions about the evidence that the case should have been dismissed immediately but at times of mass paranoia people hear what they wish to hear. In October 1678 Oates appeared before the House of Commons and named the five Lords. He was a superb actor. The Lords were arrested, charged with treason and sent to the Tower. On 10 April 1679 they were summoned to the House of Lords to answer the charges and all pleaded Not Guilty. The trials were due to begin in Westminster Hall on 13 May, as a great public spectacle, but the King's conscience was stirred and he dissolved Parliament.

This gave Henry time to prepare his defence speech and his notes for it are still with the family papers:[10]

My Lords,

I confess my Lords, it is with no Little amazement and trouble that I appear before ye Lords in the circumstances I am in, having the misfortune to be charged with a crime I have all my life time so industriously declined and I hope given sufficient testimonies of my abhorrence of it, having sacrificed my blood and fortune in the service of the King and the Crown and the preservation of the government. And to be now, in the closing of my days with such horrid designs ageynst them all is a wonder able to shake and dampen the spirits of a younger and much wiser man than myself.

My Lords, were my life only at steak it would hardly worth any men seeking and were it not for Justice and Truth's sake, scarce worth my defending; but to have my honour and Loyalty (the two things I have ever valued myself upon and preferred before my Life), to have I say, them upon so groundless a malice persecuted by such obscure men whose faces I never saw nor whose names I never heard of but upon this occasion, is a misfortune I could hardly have expected.

I am a weak, old man who is totally ignorant in the Law and unskilled in the method of managing a defence of this nature . . .

Henry's notes then contain the points he wishes to make:

No one is safe if any wicked person can swear an oath and be believed without any other evidence; if people can be convicted merely on the oath of one witness it will open the door for any evil person to use that method to prevent the course of justice; why believe Oates when you wouldn't believe the testimony of someone saying he had heard someone promising to create someone a peer; previously Oates swore an oath accusing a person guilty of a buggery[11] but witnesses

proved it was not true; he was and is a false witness. Questions for
Oates: When were you and I acquainted? In what language was the
Pope's commission written? What letters can you produce about it?

In November 1680, over a year later, Lord Stafford was summoned
to trial in a new session of Parliament. He was chosen first because there
were most witnesses against him. He was found guilty and beheaded on
29 December. Arundell's trial was due to begin the next day but the King
once again intervened by dissolving Parliament and Arundell's speech
was never made. The prisoners remained in the Tower for another
three years until February 1684. Meanwhile, many innocent men were
persecuted, many were put on trial and 35 were executed, making this
one of the most disgraceful outbreaks of mob hysteria in English history.
In May 1684 Oates was arrested and kept in prison on perjury charges.
He was eventually tried and imprisoned for life after spending a day
being pelted with rotten eggs and fruit in the pillory in Palace Yard. The
King himself died on 6 February 1685, one day after being received into
the Catholic Church by Father Huddleston.

The new King, James II had a short reign of only 46 months.
Although he promised to maintain the status quo in Church and State,
he clearly wanted to establish the Catholic Church on the same basis as
the Anglican and to remove all penalties for Catholics. Unfortunately
he lacked most of the political skill and subtlety of his brother. He was
as rigid as Charles was pliable. The new King was openly Catholic and
declined to take Anglican communion as part of his coronation. Some
people noticed that at the ceremony the crown slipped on his head and
this was taken to be an ominous sign.

Henry Arundell must have thought that at the age of 80 he was
too old to serve at Court but in July 1686 he was made a Privy Councillor
and in March 1687 he was appointed Lord Privy Seal. It is a great pity that
he did not keep a diary of events from his ringside seat. He must have
been party to discussions about keeping a standing army and employing

Catholic officers in it and about the Declaration of Indulgence when the King suspended the Penal Laws and issued edicts of toleration to all Dissenters. All the State papers record about him is that in May 1687 the King issued a warrant to the Clerk of the Signet to pay Henry at the rate of four shillings per day and not in the medieval form of sixteen dishes of fresh meat per day.

In April 1687 William of Orange, the King's son-in-law, sent an ominous message that he did not support the suspension of the Penal Laws. Then in June 1688 came sensational news from the palace. The Queen gave birth to a son after fifteen years of childless marriage. The prospect that James's potentially short reign might turn into a long-lived dynasty frightened the Protestant Establishment. Rumours spread that the baby had been smuggled into the Queen's bedroom in a warming pan. On 22 October 1688 Henry was summoned to an extraordinary Council meeting at which the Queen Dowager, who had been present at the birth, swore on oath that the baby was the Queen's own child. Henry and the others present then swore that they agreed with this.

Events were moving fast. On 5 November William of Orange landed with his army at Torbay and began a triumphant march to London. On 22 December the House of Lords ordered all Papists to leave London if they were not normally resident there and to stay within five miles of their homes. James II fled to France. Perhaps Henry welcomed the opportunity to live quietly in the country at last. He deserved a rest and perhaps time to add to the poetry he had written in the Tower.[12] No Arundell in the future would hold such a high position in government.

7

Good Marriages

THE definition of a good marriage depends on the people involved and society's expectations of marriage, but for aristocratic families the words dowry, heiress and fertility have usually been prominent. In order to maintain a position of power, an aristocratic family always expected the heir to marry someone who brought wealth to the family and the chance of a good number of children. The line must continue. There was seldom any element of the modern search for sexual and emotional satisfaction. Aristocrats had arranged marriages, as strict as those of Indian families today.

But the problem for a Catholic family, like the Arundells, was that the bride had to be Catholic too and that much reduced the choice and the likelihood of a great fortune. Land was always the bedrock of an aristocratic family's status and power but an infusion of new money was beneficial at regular intervals. One of the main sources of new money was government office but that path was closed to Catholic families. There could never have been a Catholic who amassed the wealth of Robert Walpole.[1] He built and furnished the palatial Houghton Hall from the profits of government offices over more than 30 years and also provided his three sons with large incomes for life from the government sinecures he gave them.[2]

However, in the years between 1691 and 1763 the Arundells made three good, lucrative marriages that provided the wealth for Henry,

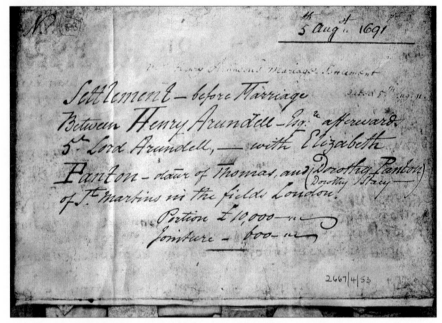

The marriage settlement of Henry Arundell and Elizabeth Panton in 1691.

the 8th Lord to build a new mansion at Wardour and thereby fall into catastrophic debt.

The first marriage in 1691 was between Henry the 5th Lord and Elizabeth Panton, daughter of Colonel Thomas Panton, the most successful gambler at the court of Charles II. He was the son of a squire from Ashby de la Zouche who moved to London in 1660 and was commissioned as a captain in the Foot Guards. He rose to be a colonel but resigned in 1667 when he converted to Catholicism. He had developed a passion for gambling and decided that henceforth he would live by his wits and luck. He was very extravagant, lived in style near the Court and kept four or five footmen 'in good liveries.' His amorous exploits were the talk of London.

Col. Panton's great skill lay in the game of Basset[3] but he was successful too with many other card games such as L'Ombre, Picquet, Gleek and Lanterloo. He won a fortune from the Dukes of Monmouth and Lauderdale and from the King's mistress, Miss Mary Davis.[4] On one occasion she announced she would limit herself to one game only but, knowing she had a bag full of gold coins, Col. Panton placed her with her back against a looking glass and he won over £1,100 in gold that night. The extraordinary and unusual quality that Panton brought to gambling was that he knew when to stop. One day he suddenly decided that he would never handle dice or cards again but would invest his winnings in buying fields in the parish of St. Martins and in building himself a grand house in the Haymarket. This was the origin of the Panton fortune which was inherited by the Arundells in the 1750s.

Col. Thomas Panton, the most successful gambler at the court of King Charles II and London property owner.

Col. Panton died in 1681 and was buried in Westminster Abbey. He left a formidable widow, Dorothy and two children, Elizabeth and her brother Thomas, who joined the army as he was not a Catholic. In 1681 Elizabeth and her mother left England to live at the French court.[5] There in 1689, Benedetto Gennari painted her as St. Catherine, holding a martyr's palm and seated next to the wheel on which the saint's body was broken for refusing to abandon her Christian faith. This was a popular pose and the Queen and even Barbara Villiers, the King's mistress, were painted in this guise. The painting,[6] now in the Tate Britain Gallery, was sent back to England, perhaps to show Elizabeth's availability for marriage. It worked and in 1691 she married Henry the 5th Lord and brought with her a £10,000 dowry (£1 million in 2010 values) and an income of £600

Elizabeth Panton, heiress to her father's fortune and wife of the 5th Lord Arundell; depicted as St. Catherine by Benedetto Gennari in 1685. (Tate, London)

a year. Her brother survived to become the oldest general in the British army, dying in 1753, and since he had never married, the whole Panton estate went to the Arundells on his death.

There is a frustrating lack of archive material about the London property, presumably because the papers were transfered when the property left the main family's ownership in 1817. It was minute compared with the Grosvenor family's inheritance of 500 acres from

The 5th Lord and Lady Arundell with their family, supposedly painted by James Maubert, shortly before Lady Arundell's death in 1708.

Sir Thomas Grosvenor's marriage to Miss Mary Davies in 1677 but it produced a good income. A 1772 Repairs Survey lists 140 Arundell–owned houses in the Strand, Norfolk Street and Arundell Street. A map dated 1810 shows the much smaller size of the property after half was sold in 1810 to meet the 8th Lord's debts. That left just over one acre but it was a golden acre because it was near Piccadilly Circus where the land was the most valuable in London. It was diverted from the owners of Wardour Castle by the 9th Lord who left it to the children of his second marriage at his death in 1817. This was a cause of great grievance in the family for many years. When I asked the last Lord's sister in 1989

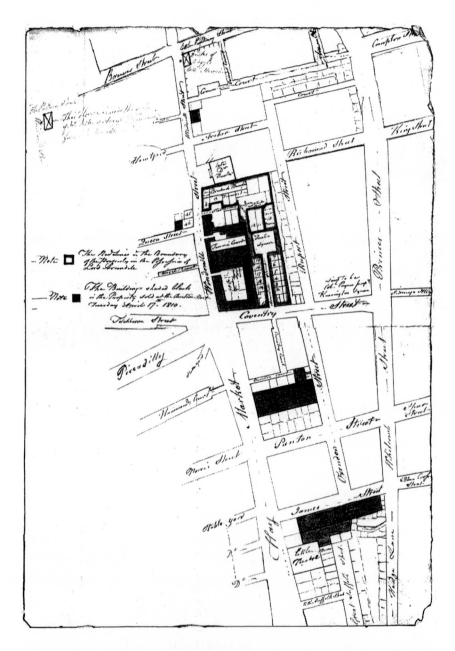

The only known map of the London estate, brought to the Arundells by Elizabeth Panton, as it was before half was sold in April 1810.

what she thought to be the cause of the family's financial troubles she said 'Losing the London property was the final straw.' The descendants of the 9th Lord's second marriage sold the whole London estate in 1915 for £250,000 (£19 million in 2010 money). It was then producing an annual income of £9,000 (£½ million) a year.[7]

The second good marriage was in 1739 when the 7th Lord married his distant cousin from Cornwall, Mary Bellings-Arundell. She was the descendant of the 16th century Thomas the Founder's older brother John. It was by no means certain that she would become a great heiress because she had an older sister Frances who married and would probably produce children. In fact Frances was left widowed and childless in 1737 and died in 1752, leaving her sister as sole heiress to the Cornish property with its lucrative tin mines. Mary brought a £10,000 dowry to the marriage (worth £1.5 million in 2010) as well as the prospect of the Cornish estate.

When Henry the 8th Lord inherited the title and the Wardour estates in 1756 he was only sixteen but a very rich man, from his own estates and in expectation of the Cornish estates when his mother died. They all came to him unencumbered by entails so that he could do as he liked with them. There was no settlement to protect the estates and keep them in the family. Every banker and moneylender in London must have waited in joyful anticipation. As Dr. Johnson wrote in 1780:

> Wealth, my lad, was made to wander,
> Let it wander as it will.
> See the jockey, see the pander,[8]
> Bid them come and take their fill.
>
> Call the Bettys, Kates and Jennies,
> Every name that laughs at care;
> Lavish of your grandsire's guineas,
> Show the spirit of an heir.

Unfortunately we have very little information about Mary Bellings-Arundell except for a few letters that she wrote to the agent at Wardour, old Haylock, in the late 1750s and early 1760s and to her lawyers in London and Axminster.[9] The fact that these letters have survived is probably because they deal with business and not just with family news and London gossip. Lady Arundell was living at her house in Old Burlington Street, London and at a rented house near Maidenhead. It is worth quoting from a few of the letters for the glimpses they give us of Wardour and the family in the mid 18th century. Lady Arundell's spelling and punctuation have been retained except that 'f' has been changed to 's' where appropriate.

The first letter to old Haylock at Wardour is dated 30 May 1758, two years after Mary was widowed. It is all about horses; not paying too much for a servant's horses and ordering Will Penney to come up to London with 'three Coach Horses and the two saddle horses'. The letter ends, 'you may order in Chickens and Ducks to fatt as usual.' Nearly a year later on 17 March 1759 another letter to Haylock begins with instructions about engaging a new servant at Wardour, Thomas Barber, 'a good, strong young man and sightly' at £5 a year wages and five shillings a week 'bord wages.' There had been some confusion over Haylock's wages which Lady Arundell confirms at £34 a year 'for everything' but there had been 'want of money in my late Lord's time.' A change was about to happen– 'now at Lady Day you will begin everything upon my son's account' so Henry at the age of eighteen was about to take control, although he was still absent on the Grand Tour. The letter ends with instructions to tell the gardener that he need not keep the garden, 'coped[10] upon my account as my Stay at Wardour will be short, only when I am wanted upon Business. I shall chuse to have the Gardens kept neate and not run to rune but not all the expense it was last year.'

A letter to her London lawyer, Purser, on 31 May 1759 reveals her concern about her son taking over the estate. She had written to Henry, still travelling in Europe:

Mary Bellings-Arundell, unexpectedly sole heiress of the vast Arundell estates in Cornwall and wife of her seventh cousin, the 7th Lord Arundell, painted by George Knapton in the 1740s.

I told him his Estate would not afford to spend so much and that I could not tell exactly what he would have yearly, but hoped when all charges was payed he wou'd have £1,000 for I thought it best to tell him to little as I find his inclination is so much for spending Money.

Perceptive woman; she obviously recognised the signs of extravagance in her son. A year later, another letter to Purser asks for money:

I shou'd not be so pressing only for the reasons I mentioned to you in my last for I am as saving as I can at present in not spending more than is necessary till I have paid what I owe the tradespeople . . . I was very much fatigued yesterday at being at Mr. Arundell's Wedding and going into the Cold Church did not agree with me at all but I did not know how to refuse them as they desired it so much my being at it; I think its a very bad match on both sides.[11]

The next letter on 7 May 1761 to her agent and lawyer in Axminster is full of financial arrangements:

I was in hopes before now to let you know of my Son's arrival. I had a letter coming from him yesterday from St. Omers dated ye 27 of last month that he proposed to set out the next Day so hope he will be here soon, he says he will writ to me as soon as he lands he says his Brother has had a cold and sore throat but is now very well again so hope he is set out for Laflech by this time, for Mr. Church who is to go with him has drawn on me for a £100 which I suppose is to Ecquip him for his Journey as he will want everything coming out of the college, after that I shall let him know they must not exceed £100 a year while he is at the College of Laflech . . . so the paying out the £400 to my Eldest Son and this £100 for Tomey's use it has distressed me very much at present as I have nothing coming to me out of the last money you sent to Mr. Wright[12] so shall be very glad if you cou'd send me some soon for my own use as I have only forty pound of those Bills left . . . I am Loath to ask you for money as you

Henry and Thomas Arundell, children of the 7th Lord by an unknown artist in the early 1750s.

always send it as soon as you can get it but another year I shall not want it so much as my Edest Son will be on his own footing and see what he has to spend; as to myself I am as frugal as I can, I want to pay my coach maker a £100 which has been a long time standing not that he is in a hurry for it, its for my Post Chaise . . .

There was good news on 23 May 1761 in another letter to her Axminster agent:

I have the pleasure to acquaint you of my Sons Safe arrival last Saturday about four o'clock; he had a very good passage; only about four Houres; he's very Tall and Lufty; but think I shou'd have known him anywhere; next week he designes going to Salisbury; to pay a visit to his Uncles[13] and to go to Wardour for two or three days, just to see the place, but not to stay; and I have advised him to go to Bath to see his aunt there in his way back as she longs so much to see him.

Five days later Haylock at Wardour received this letter:

I sent by the Waggon yesterday a Dozen Knives and forks, Green Handles as allso Eleven Silver spoons for you have one Spoon at Wardour, which makes up a Dozen as there is not any knives and forks at Wardour[14]. I send them down for my sons use; and you will take care and put them by when he comes away; the Box will be in Salisbury tonight.

The reply from Haylock is dated 3 June 1761:

Madam, I had the Honour of your Ladyship's Letter by Saturdays Post and have Ever since Honoured with waiting on his Lordship and Company or other ways should have answered it before, his Lordship and two Mr Arundells[15] kame hear Saturday to dinner and the Mr. Arundells has bin hear til this Morning his Lordship set of for Bath in Good Health which Pray God continues he is the finest Man I ever saw and is admired by all that saw him his Sweet Temper and regular life is Suth as is Justly the admiration of Everybody and are virtues rare to be found. His Lordship and Company never drank more than one Bottle of Wine after super and went up every Night at Aleven, Ris early in the morning and went to Mr. Barnses Monday and to Ashcombe[16] yesterday and returned both days to Dinner. I ham sory the seson will not produce game which if could have bin had ould have bin a great help but hops his Lordship's Goodness will exques all Falts. The Knives and forks and a dozen spones Kame safely Fryday by Short, I have consulted Mr. Walker about the young

Hors and he says if he is turned out thear is no danger . . . Will Penny
is Gon with my Lord and the Scothman is left hear, I have given Will
Penny a strict charge to keep sober and he has promised to dow it and
I ham in great hopes he will be as Good as his promis he has behaved
very well at Wardour . . .

There are only a few more letters in this bundle and it is clear
that Lady Arundell found it difficult to relinquish control over estate
business. In August 1761 she arranged for Henry to 'Register his Estate'[17]
and remarked that he was definitely going to attend the Coronation[18] but
was not certain whether she would go with him. Will Penny continued
to be a problem and she wrote to Haylock in September 1761, 'Pray tell
William Penny that I am extremely angry with him, and if he do drink he
will not do for my Son but as you tell me he shows so much repentance
I have not for this time told my son of it . . . '

On 21 February 1769 Lady Arundell died, leaving her son a
fortune. He put this notice in the London papers:

This morning the corps of the late Rt Hon Lady Dowager Arundell
was carried from her house in Grosvenor Street to his Lordship's seat
at Wardour Castle in Wiltshire there to lay in State and to be buried
with ye remains of the late Lord her husband in ye family vault at
Tisbury.

The third lucrative marriage was Henry the 8th Lord's marriage
to Maria Christina Conquest in 1763. She was an heiress from Irnham
in Lincolnshire and brought to the family a small estate of about
2,000 acres and a fine house at Irnham. She appears to have been as
careful as Henry was profligate Although none of her letters survives,
her household account books[19] do and several pages record her visit
to Hotwells Spa in Bristol in July and August 1786 with her daughter
Laura.[20] Every penny was accounted for.

Hotwells Spa had a short period of great popularity in the middle and later years of the 18th century and then suddenly declined because charges became exorbitant when the owners needed to rebuild the quay walls. The spa water gushed out of an opening on the edge of the river Avon. This tidal river, busy with ships and full of the waste of England's second largest city, made the water difficult to access and the stink from the river at low tide was always a problem. When the Arundells were visiting, a Master of Ceremonies had been newly appointed. He ensured that no swords or spurs were worn in the Pump Room and he supervised the daily routine in the surrounding rooms – drinking the water, playing cards, listening to the orchestra and promenading along the river bank. In the evenings there were receptions and balls. The water was warm, sparkling and especially recommended for those 'who have hot livers, feeble brains and red pimply faces.'[21] Other visitors believed it to be a cure for diabetes and T.B. It also made excellent tea.

We do not know exactly where the Arundells stayed but it was probably in a house on College Green or in Dowry Square. The following are some of the entries in Lady Arundell's account book.

Money Spent by Me on My Daughter Laura's Account	£	s.	d.
Laura's Washing by her Maid for 7 weeks	2	7	4 ½
Laura's Subscription to the Master of Ceremonies Ball	I	I	O
Laura's Milliner's Bill	I	I	39
For two Pairs of Shoes for Laura		18	O
Two yards of fine Muslin for a Cloak for Laura	2	10	O
To the Moravians for Working above in Tambour[22]	2	12	6
Gave Dr. Renandot for his First and Last visit	2	2	O
To the Pump Woman and Men + for Water	2	2	O
A Ganse Cup for Laura when Sick		4	6
Laura's Shoemaker's Bill at Bath[23]	9	2	O
The Dentist Fox for Laura	I	I	O

The Dentist at Bath	10	6
Bristol Week and Day Bills		
Paid James Barry the Apothecary	11	2
Paid for two pounds of Coffee	7	0
Paid for a Sack of Coals		11
Paid for a Turkey and a Chicken	4	11
Paid for 2 lbs of Butter	1	8
Paid John Papps the Butchers Bill	21 5	4
Paid John Simson for Bottles	3 2	6
Paid Georges Morgan the Pastry Cook	4 14	3
Paid to Davis for Garden Stuff	2 7	5
Paid for a place in the Bristol Coach to Bath	3	0
Paid to James Rogers for Fetching Water 16 days	8	0
Paid to a Carpenter for nailing Boxes and Loading Cart	2	6
Paid for the road from Bath to Wardour	6	6

The whole account is carefully totalled and checked and signed. The grand total came to £174 . 16 . 6 ½d, leaving £90 . 13 . 5 ½ d from the money 'received of my Lord from our going to Bristol.'

One is left with the impression that if Maria Christina and her mother-in-law, two careful women, had been in charge of the Arundell estates while Henry indulged his passion for building and collecting pictures on an allowance they gave him, the decline and fall of Wardour might not have happened.

8

Henry the Magnificent

WHEN Henry Arundell succeeded his father as the 8th Lord Arundell in 1756, at the age of sixteen, he joined a small exclusive group. During the whole of the 18th century, no more than 1,003 people held peerages or, in the memorable words of Professor John Cannon, 'considerably less than the pupils at most comprehensive schools and distinctly less than the attendance at Darlington football club on a wet Saturday in February.' But Henry belonged within the peerage to an even smaller group, that of the Catholic peers. There were only six of them in 1800[1].

For these aristocratic families, the owners of great landed estates, political power and status were the normal accompaniment of their wealth. They built vast country mansions to give physical expression to their political power or the search for it. But the Catholic peers were shut out from political power and influence by the various Penal Laws which barred them from political office, both locally and nationally. For them, the ownership of a country mansion might have seemed almost unnecessary since there was no possibility of exercising political power. But a country mansion also represented social status and style. It was what everyone expected from a great landowner, Catholic or Protestant.

The Arundells had lived for a hundred years since the Civil War in a small house under the bailey wall at Wardour, in a rented house at Breamore in Hampshire and in London. It is perhaps surprising that

The 8th Lord by George Romney. The painting is at Ugbrooke Park, the home of his son-in-law Lord Clifford. (Photographic Survey, The Courtauld Institute of Art)

Henry's major contribution to family history was the building of a vast, new mansion at Wardour, before political power for Catholics became a reality at the time of emancipation in 1829.[2] Did he perhaps foresee that the abolition of the Penal Laws was not far distant and did he want to set

A south east view of the new castle engraved by J. Buckler and printed in Colt Hoare's History of Modern Wiltshire *in 1829.*

up the family with the apparatus to play their part on the national stage? Or was it simply that he was the first Arundell with sufficient resources to build on a major scale? There is obviously an irresistible compulsion for a man who becomes extremely rich to build a big house, beyond the needs of a normal family.

How much wiser he would have been to continue to live in a small house such as Old Wardour House or Hook Manor, across the Park at Wardour, and to concentrate instead on developing the wealth of the family from their tin mines in Cornwall, their vast agricultural estates and their lucrative acres in London.[3] But that would have required extraordinary frugality and eccentricity. A great mansion was the normal accessory of a great estate and spoke of the social prestige and position of a family.[4] Not to build one if you didn't already possess one, was to let down the side and to appear as strange as a king without a crown.

We know very little about Henry as a person because almost none of his personal letters survives and his journal appears to have been destroyed except for a few pages from 1787. He was extremely tall, six feet six inches according to the sacristan at Wardour who measured him for his coffin. Contemporaries described him as kind and generous and this is confirmed by his lenient attitude to the financial problems of his brother Thomas.[5] He was also extremely loyal. His old teacher, Father Booth, spent his last eighteen years as a guest at Wardour. Henry's handwriting is large and flowing which to graphologists indicates an open-hearted personality. But he was not a good organiser if his account books are compared with those of his wife who was meticulous.

Henry's main problem was procrastination. The letters of Richard Woods, who supervised the landscaping of the Park at Wardour in the 1760s, are full of pleas that Henry should 'make up his mind' and reach a clear decision about this plan or that proposal. It was like trying to get water from a stone. Henry was educated by the Jesuits at St. Omers in France from 1753 to 1758 and in the latter year he set out on the Grand Tour with his old teacher Father Charles Booth, 'a man of very good sense, a Jesuit, but without any of their absurd prejudices', according to a contemporary Scottish resident in Italy.[6] Whatever the skills of Father Booth, they did not include teaching his pupil good financial record keeping. Henry began an account book at the start of the Tour but filled only 12 pages

Henry 8th Lord Arundell painted in Rome while he was on the Grand Tour in the late 1750s.

Maria Christina Conquest by Giles Hussey (1710-1788). She was heiress to the Conquest estates at Irnham in Lincolnshire and as careful as her husband was profligate. (National Portrait Gallery, London)

and then lost interest, a pattern that was to be repeated in later life where money was concerned. He visited Paris, Genoa, Florence, Rome and Parma and spent a year at the Turin Academy.

In May 1763, Henry married Mary Conquest from Irnham in Lincolnshire. She was an heiress but not on the scale of his mother. She brought to the marriage the invaluable qualities of sobriety, constancy and fortitude. In the portrait by Giles Hussey[7] she shows all the hallmarks of a good housekeeper. Henry signed his accounts once a year as if he were signing an oil painting; she checked, altered and signed her Household Accounts every month. The couple had three children, all daughters; Mary, Eleanora and Anna, who lived for only a year. A son was greatly longed for but despite the prayers of the Pope in the 1770s, no more children were born. After 1776 the couple made Wardour their main home but there were frequent visits to London and Irnham. Wherever they lived, they had a reputation for 'unbounded hospitality' and George Oliver wrote that 'Catholics and Protestant were equally welcome at their table.'[8]

It is not easy to calculate Henry's wealth as there does not appear to have been any central accounting procedure for his income. Samuel Angier began the magnificent calf-bound ledgers in 1778 but they relate only to the Wardour estate and sometimes appear to be more an exercise in fine calligraphy than financial recording.[9] Henry undoubtedly came into the category of 'great landlord' as described by Joseph Massie, the economist, in 1760. These were men with an income of at least £20,000 a year from land. Henry's income from his estates was £35,000 a year (£4.5 million in 2010 values) and rising. He had estates in London (2 acres), Wiltshire (22,052 acres), North Dorset (6,599 acres), South Dorset (3,000 acres), Somerset (about 1,200 acres), Lincolnshire (4,000 acres), Hampshire (1,684 acres) and Cornwall (not recorded).[10] The estates were an entrepreneur's dream – not only the solid agricultural bedrock but the lucrative urban property in London and the tin mines in Cornwall.[11] Good management by an energetic agent such as was employed on the Holkham estate for the Cokes[12] or the Trentham estate for the Leveson-Gowers would have ensured the status of 'great landowner' remained as such for generations to come. But there was no professional agent at Wardour.

Unfortunately, Henry had no precedents to guide him in the management of such vast estates. The London property did not come

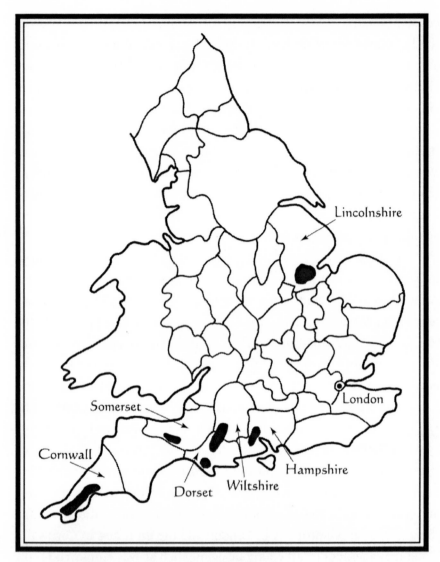

The location of all the Arundell estates at their greatest extent c. 1770.

to the family fully until the death of Elizabeth Panton's brother, General Panton in 1751, a few years before Henry's father died. The vast Cornish estates (26 manors and tin and copper mines) were not the property of the Wardour Arundells until Henry's aunt Frances, Lady Gifford died childless in 1752. There had been no time for consolidation before Henry inherited them. The Lincolnshire estate was officially Lady Arundell's until her death but it was yet another property to be administered from a distance of several hundred miles. There were seven estates in eight counties. At least Henry's income was not complicated by the 'snug sinecures' which most noblemen expected from their involvement in politics. Henry simply had the income from his estates but that was enough to put him in the category of the richest in the land. It was a magnificent inheritance.

Yet in 1798, ten years before he died, Henry faced bankruptcy. When all his debts were calculated they came to £327,673 (£31.5 million) and Henry had achieved the unenviable position of contender for the title of 'Biggest Bankrupt of the 18th century'. His financial affairs were put in the hands of trustees,[13] his bank account at Hoare's bank was closed and opened again with a small income, controlled by the trustees (his sons-in-law).[14] All his estates were put up for sale except a small part of the Wardour estate and half the London estate – almost all the land in Cornwall, all the mines, all the land in Dorset, Somerset and Hampshire. It was a spectacular disaster.

C A S E,

Submitted to Sir V. GIBBS, His Majesty's Solicitor-General, and Messrs. RICHARDS, HARGRAVE, and SHADWELL, Barristers at Law.

General Statement of the Affairs of Lord Arundell.

	Principal Sums and Interest.			Annuities per Annum.		
	£.	s.	d.	£.	s.	d.
THE number of Mortgages and Family Portions charged upon his Lordship's estates is 28, amounting, with interest due thereon, to about	150,800	0	0			
Judgments affecting the estates, in number about 16, amounting, with interest, to about	24,000	0	0			
The Annuitants specific and by judgment are in number about 43, amounting to, per annum				5,113	12	6
The Annuitants by Bond are 60 in number, amounting per annum to				3,468	0	0
Arrears of Annuities, and accruing interests, about	10,000	0	0			
Bond-Debts, in number 80, and interest, amounting to about	58,472	0	0			
Simple contract debts	6,927	0	0			
	£250,099	0	0	£8,581	12	6

	£.	s.	d.
The annual outgoings for interest of monies and payment of annuities, are upwards of	17,000	0	0
The income in any way derivable from the estates of his Lordship is short of	7,000	0	0 per Ann.
The annual deficiency, above,	£10,000	0	0

The resources of Lord *Arundell* are valued altogether at about £400,000, and it is supposed will yield a surplus to his Lordship, after payment of all his debts, of from £60,000 to £70,000.

The estates are vested in Trustees, in Trust, to sell and pay the creditors having specific securities :— To the completion of sales which have already been made, and of others in contemplation, the only difficulty arises from the number of persons having specific securities and liens by Judgment upon them ; and it is found impracticable to obtain the concurrence of so many persons in the different Conveyances to the different purchasers ; and many of the contracts will be rescinded, unless the Trustees are enabled, without loss of time, to carry these contracts into execution :—It is for these reasons proposed to call a meeting of the Mortgage, Judgment, and Annuitant creditors, and in the mean time to submit to them the annexed proposal.

Under these circumstances, you are requested to give your Opinion on the affairs of Lord *Arundell*, and consider the propriety of the annexed proposal.

Statement before the Solicitor-General of the financial catastrophe facing the 8th Lord in 1800.

In one generation, the Arundells fell from the position of great landowners, on a par in their wealth with dukes and earls, to the level of ordinary Wiltshire squires, although the title of Lord Arundell and the mansion at Wardour remained as a reminder of better days. Worst of all, Henry was sentenced to imprisonment in the Marshalsea, the notorious debtors' prison in Southwark. However, a note in the family archives says that he avoided imprisonment by claiming privilege of peerage. This gave freedom from arrest in civil cases and meant that a peer could demand to be tried by his fellow peers in the House of Lords. It was abolished in 1948.

PARTICULARS

of the

MANOR OF FONTMELL,

Extending over about 2030 Acres (including Bedchester) of rich Land, with a fine Trout Stream, and sundry valuable Mills thereon, with the Right to Court Leet, at which the Officers of the several Parishes within the Hundred of Sixpenny are appointed ;

THE MANOR, OR REPUTED MANOR, OF

HARTGROVE,

Extending over 785 Acres ;

THE MANOR, OR REPUTED MANOR, OF

WEST ORCHARD,

Extending over 638 Acres ;

(N. B. These last Manors are now Portof the Manor of Fontmell, but intended to be sold separately, with the Manorial Rights thereon.)

THE MANOR OF

COMPTON ABBAS, WITH TWYFORD,

Extending over 1900 Acres, or thereabouts,

WITH THE ADVOWSON IN FEE OF THE RECTORY, AND THE RIGHT TO GREAT AND SMALL TYTHES;

ALSO THE

MANOR OF MELBURY ABBAS,

Extending over upwards of 2500 Acres ;

AND THE ADVOWSON IN FEE OF THE RECTORY OF

MELBURY ABBAS,

WITH THE GREAT AND SMALL TYTHES,

AND ALSO THE REVERSION IN FEE OF SEVERAL

Leasehold and Copyhold Estates,

Held by Lives within the said Manors.

The whole composed of rich Grazing Ground, Arable Lands and Downs, near the Centre of which is that remarkable Hill, called

MELBURY HILL,

SITUATED IN THE NEIGHBOURHOOD OF SHAFTSBURY,

IN THE

COUNTY OF DORSET,

WHICH WILL BE SOLD BY AUCTION,

By MESSRS. HODSKINSON, ABBOTT, AND Co.

At GARRAWAY's, on WEDNESDAY, the 9th of MAY, 1805

IN FIVE LOTS.

Printed Particulars may be had of Mr. Bowles, Solicitor, Shaftsbury ; Mr. Abbott, Shepherd's-Market ; and at Messrs. Hodskinsons, Arundel-Street, London, where Plans of the Estates may be seen.

Sale particulars of Arundell estates in North Dorset in 1805, made necessary by the 8th Lord's debts.

Henry's reaction to his bankruptcy is not known. It is unlikely that he would have echoed Sheridan's words when he saw a friend paying his creditors: 'Paying creditors? What a waste! What a waste!' He was a kind and generous man, as we know from his attitude to his brother's debts in the 1770s. He often said he would pay his creditors in full. He was genuinely puzzled by his problems. 'There's a dearth of money about' is a favourite expression, as if money was a commodity like eggs or corn, unrelated to his own credit worthiness. In a bundle of Henry's letters from 1803 the word 'mortified' leaps from the page. Perhaps this is the moment of contrition. No, he is mortified that creditors who promised to wait another year for payment have run out of patience and will take him to court. In the end, most of the estates were sold to pay his debts and there is no reason to suppose the money did not reach his creditors eventually. But his grandson was still trying to pay the debts twenty years later, as new claims appeared.

The process by which a person becomes bankrupt is not easy to follow. It is not in the nature of a spendthrift to keep careful accounts. Henry was no different. The 250 letters to his agent in London, John Purser,[15] are all about borrowing money, not spending it. The following on 19 March 1774, is typical:

> Sir,
> Seeing ye inclos'd advertisement of one who has £6,000 to lend on Bond, I wish you wou'd enquire about it today, and if he will lend it on Bond, or if he objects to it on Bond, chargeable on any of the Manors. I wou'd not have ye mention my Name yet, but ye may tell him ye person has estates out of settlement wh. produce between £8,000 & £9,000 & if requir'd he may see ye settlements and other powers . . . Advertisement : A Gentleman who has about £6,000 in the stocks would be glad to lend the whole or any part of it to a Gentleman of Character on his bond . . .

Henry borrowed money by bond, by mortgage, by annuities and by straight loans as much and as often as he could so that by 1794, the annual interest payments on his debts were 51% of his total income. By 1800 they were over 80%. Henry was not unique in facing this problem. Debt and landowners went together like a carriage and horses. Thomas Coke of Holkham owed £91,000 in 1759, the Earl Grosvenor owed £150,000 in 1777, Sir William St. Quinton £126,000 in 1785. The big difference was that all these and most other landowners' debts were managed successfully before permanent damage was inflicted on the family estates, which were usually protected from one generation's profligacy by entails.[16] The Arundell estates were unprotected and never recovered from Henry's extravagance.

One small collection of 37 letters[17] throws some light on Henry's failure to control his borrowing. James Knight was the family's agent on the small Somerset and South Dorset estate. His letters to Henry in the late 1790s explain his frustration with his employer. In the first letter he told Henry that the bank at Bridgwater was demanding repayment of a £3,000 loan and would accept no delay. Henry could not provide any money so Knight used £600 of his own money as part payment, 'money I had been saving up to place out my Eldest son in business . . . and 10 children all of whom are now become expensive to me.' He mentioned that his Lordship owed him another £4,000 on Bond but, deferential as ever, he ended, 'I wd. take my Trouble sooner than putt your Lordship to any Inconvenience.' Over the next few months the Bank's demands became more insistent. Knight tried to add lives to tenants' leases to raise money but Henry's only response was to ask for more loans. Knight replied with appropriate deference :'I will use my Utmost Endeavours to raise what Money I can here . . . I have little Hopes to obtain it for your Lordship, there's such a Scarcity of Money at this time.'

Knight suggested a survey of all the estates to ensure that farms were let at maximum rent but nothing was done. The opportunity for debt to act as a trigger for economic development in agriculture or mining was thus lost. One of the last letters in 1801 shows Knight's desperation:

> What can I do my Lord? I have not the money and have assured you I will not borrow it, I have lost my Creditt nearly by borrowing and applying to my Friends for Money for your Use and if you are determined my Lord to go on contracting of Debts without thinking of payment you must think me worse than a Brute to ruin my own children to pay your Debts.

In the following years all the farms Knight had looked after were put up for sale.

We need to look more closely at the pre-conditions and direct causes of Henry's bankruptcy. There are no easy answers but of greatest significance in the background was undoubtedly the fact that many of the Arundell estates were 'out of settlement' as Henry mentioned in his letter to Purser. The law of settlement is immensely complicated. It is said that only six people have ever understood it fully and this author is not one of them. At its most basic it means that if a 'strict settlement' is made in every generation, a family's land is protected from an individual's reckless extravagance. It is, in the words of Edmund Burke, 'a partnership not only between those who are living but between those who are living, those who are dead and those who are yet to be born.'

Most of Henry's estates were held by him 'in fee simple', that is they were his to dispose of as he wished. They could be sold to raise cash whenever there was a crisis. They were a creditor's dream. The fact that settlements had broken down on Henry's estates was due to medical and genetic factors. In 1739 when his father married Mary Bellings-Arundell, the Cornish heiress, a strict settlement was made between Henry's grandfather and his son, ensuring that the estates would descend 'in tail mail' to the bridegroom's eldest unborn son, i.e. Henry. The 7th Lord inherited in 1746 and would have made another strict settlement on the marriage of his eldest son but unfortunately the 7th Lord died when his son was only sixteen and Henry inherited the estates 'in fee simple'. When Henry married Mary Conquest in 1763, he made a settlement that his estates should go to 'his first and other sons of the marriage successively, according to seniority in Tail Male, on the body of Mary Conquest' but when the marriage failed to produce a son the estates reverted to Henry 'in fee simple.' In addition, Henry inherited all his mother's Cornish estates 'in fee simple' in 1769 and he never made them part of a settlement. If the estates were 'settled' they could not be touched to pay debts except by permission of an Act of

Parliament. If they were held 'in fee simple' they were available to pay debts at any time.[18]

These preconditions for Henry's bankruptcy are easy to understand but the direct causes are not. It is often believed that the building of a great mansion was the direct route to bankruptcy for any landed family. But the process may not be so simple. The actual building of New Wardour Castle, the largest Georgian mansion in Wiltshire between 1769 and 1776 should not in itself have bankrupted a man with an annual income of £35,000 (£4.5 million). There are no clear account books giving yearly totals of expenditure on the new mansion but a bewildering scattering of payments to craftsmen, (Mason's work £8,793; Plaisterers' Account £996 4s. 1½d.; Carpenters and Joiners £6,516, Plummers £424 13s. 5d., Locksmith £100).[19] However, there is a simple method of calculating the total cost of building the carcase of the new mansion. Paine's contract with Lord Arundell states that he will be architect and surveyor and make two visits to Wardour each year to supervise and check progress. His fee was 5% of the total building cost and his bank account at Coutts Bank survives for these years. He was paid a total of £2,091.5.2d for work at Wardour which gives an approximate cost for the building of £41,825.[20] Nothing to cause bankruptcy there.

Perhaps fitting out and furnishing were the greatest expense.[21] We do not have any regular accounts for this expenditure but there is some evidence for the cost of furnishings. It is very likely that the Arundells needed to furnish the mansion from scratch – there was no large collection of paintings and furniture to be transferred from elsewhere. Therefore between 1768 and 1792 Henry employed Father John Thorpe[22] as his purchasing agent in Rome. His instructions were to purchase paintings 'having always a strict regard to decency' and other works of art. Nearly 350 letters survive from Thorpe to Henry but none the other way. A typical letter is that for 27 August 1774:

My Dear Lord,

The inclosed List will tell your Lordship the contents of Three Cases now packed up and wanting for a fourth which is to contain Paintings and to be sent with them:

27 Parcels of Prints

A Madonna from Coreggio

Pope Clement XIII by Mengs

Jacob's Journey to Egypt by Poussin

A Cardinal holding a Crucifix

Henry paid Thorpe mainly from his account at Hoare's Bank and it was hoped that there would be a complete record there. In fact there are long gaps with no payments and Henry may then have been using his other account at Wright's Bank. The total paid to Thorpe and recorded in Hoare's account from 1771 to 1791 is £7,427. Nothing to cause bankruptcy there but there are no identifiable payments to furniture makers such as Chippendale or for carpets, silver and domestic items. Two silver-gilt candlesticks from Henry's collection were sold in New York recently for $50,000. If they are typical of the quality of Henry's purchases, they help to explain his financial problems. Henry's first major project was the landscaping of the Park and the total amount paid to Richard Woods was only about £5,000, a small sum in relation to total income over ten years.

Undoubtedly it is worth bearing in mind the opinion of William Bankes of Kingston Lacy who visited Wardour Castle in December 1811 and wrote to his grandmother:[23] 'His (the 9th Lord's) income is still greatly straitened by the enormous debts contracted by his predecessor in building a House quite disproportion to his fortune and feeding a train of thankless Emigrants.' Bankes himself was no stranger to extravagance and therefore his judgment should be respected. The feeding of emigrants obviously refers to Henry giving asylum to French émigré clergy who left France after the Revolution rather than take the oath that accompanied the Civil Constitution of the Clergy. About 3,000 priests sought refuge in England in the early 1790s and Henry was anxious to help. A list survives of 82 names of those staying for several years at Wardour Castle and indicates the scale of Henry's generosity. But Bed, Breakfast and Evening Meal for 82 should not have strained the resources of one of England's richest men. He also provided Coombe House in Donhead for Carthusians from Normandy, Stapehill in Dorset for Cistercian nuns and Lanherne in Cornwall for Carmelite nuns. Costs do not appear in the account books. There may have been heavy expenditure also on buildings for Catholic schools and worship in various parts of the country.

It is perhaps significant that the last Lord's sister Isabel remembered in 1989 that when she and her brother ran round the house in the 1920s, they called out 'Old Piety, Old Piety' whenever they passed a portrait of the 8th Lord. She explained that he was much too pious and 'spent too much money on his piety,' an interesting reflection of family opinion, transmitted down the generations. There is much evidence that Henry took his duties as a Catholic nobleman very seriously. Three quarters of all Catholics in Wiltshire lived on the Wardour estate in the 18th century and as the focus of this community, Henry lavished time and money on a magnificent chapel in the west wing of the new mansion. It was the largest and most splendid Catholic Church built in England since the Reformation. Father Thorpe in Rome advised on the decoration and furnishing of the chapel. It was obviously a project dear to his heart and in one of his letters he includes the intriguing message for Lord Arundell, 'the Pope never forgets his favourite English peer.' No expense was spared on the chapel and it is impossible to calculate the total cost but it must have been colossal.

Household expenses could be another severe drain on income especially as Henry and his wife had a reputation for keeping an ever-open door. An early 19th century guidebook to Wardour contrasts the welcome visitors received at Wardour with the hostility they encountered at neighbouring Fonthill Abbey under the reclusive William Beckford.[24] Lady Arundell appears to have kept meticulous accounts and the housekeeping totals averaged about £3,000 a year between 1774 and 1789. However, expenditure doubled from 1790 to 1795 due to the presence of French clergy in the castle. Residence in London was another severe drain on the resources of any family and the Arundells made frequent visits there, which included long stays in winter, but they cannot have caused a spectacular bankruptcy.[25]

What about politics? They could bankrupt a family which was heavily involved, as in the case of Coke of Norfolk (1754-1842) who spent at least £40,000 on 'costly electioneering'. But Henry played no part in national politics and never even took his seat in the House of Lords, despite the 1791 Catholic Relief Act which made provision for Catholic peers to take an acceptable oath of allegiance.

'Fast women and slow horses' were the cause of disaster for many aristocratic families. Henry was not interested in either. One remote possibility remains. The last Lord Arundell valued greatly a family heirloom, the gold pocket watch which belonged to Charles James Fox. Is it possible that this was given to Henry by Fox as recognition of friendship and support? Fox campaigned for the removal of the Penal Laws. He hated the discrimination against Catholics. But he was a compulsive gambler, dedicated to betting on cards and horses. George III called him 'the tutor in debauchery' to his son the Prince of Wales. If Henry was involved in helping to pay Fox's gambling debts there is no need to look any further for the straw that broke the camel's back. Not surprisingly, there is no record in the account books.

In the end there is no clear explanation. When the 10th Lord's brother-in-law, Richard Temple-Nugent-Brydges-Chandos-Grenville, first Duke of Buckingham died in 1839 he left debts of £355,000, slightly larger than Henry's. His widow was asked to explain how this had happened. She could not give any explanation except to say, 'He was hospitable and charitable and very expensive in his usual habits.'

The Economist commented a few years later that the Duke was 'neither a gambler, a drunkard nor a profligate.[26] So it was with Henry. His debts just grew and grew and he was too weak to take control and reduce them. Indeed, it might be said that both Henry and his brother Thomas who spent long years 'sodden and in jail' were chronic 'debtaholics'.

9

Wardour the Magnificent

IT is often said that Britain's greatest contribution to the visual arts is the country house and park. Throughout the 18th century landowners of all shapes and sizes were building new houses and laying out 'natural' parks around their houses. The old 17th century gardens with their formal designs, gravel paths and box hedges were abandoned as too artificial and too French. They looked as if the gardeners were on sentry duty and wanted everything under control. English armies had beaten the French in battle so why shouldn't the English lead the world in garden design and produce something that reflected English freedom rather than French autocracy?

The name that is forever associated with the new fashion for landscaping parks and gardens is Lancelot or Capability Brown (1716-1783). He was a genius who could so arrange trees, hills, lakes and valleys that future generations would think they were in paradise when they visited his parks. It was said of him that he had a poet's feeling and a painter's eye and 'so closely did he copy Nature that his works will be mistaken.'[1]

Henry the 8th Lord's parents employed Brown to make a survey of the deer parks at Wardour in 1754 and to provide plans for improvement. Brown charged £77 9s. 11d. for 'five whole days at Wardour and a General Plan for 620 acres'[2] but the plans do not survive and nothing was carried out. Many years later, Henry himself

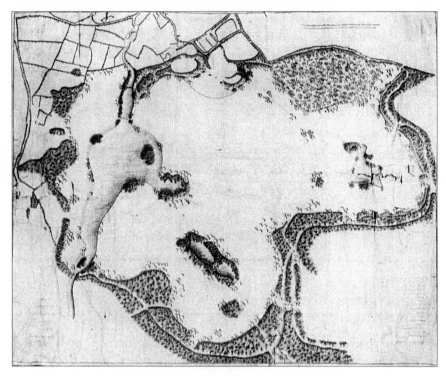

A proposal by Capability Brown for improvements at Wardour in 1775 but never carried out.

contacted Brown in August 1773 and asked him to submit proposals, 'as I am making improvements here . . .' Eventually Brown produced more plans and a map[3] showing a great lake stretching across the park and belts of trees on the hillsides. Nothing came of that scheme either, for which Brown was paid £80. It is therefore quite wrong to give Brown credit for the Wardour landscape. The man who created the park was Richard Woods (1716-1793).

Very little is known about the early years of Woods.[4] He was a Catholic and this may have brought him to Henry's attention. In 1751 he was living in Chertsey and described himself as a 'gardner'. He became a surveyor and draughtsman too and his first recorded commission was a landscape in Oxfordshire in 1758. By the time he first visited Wardour in 1764 he had worked for seven different landowners.

Woods' method of working was to make an overall plan, submit estimates for separate sections, visit the site several times a year, make contracts with local workmen and select the best plants and seeds from London nurseries. He always needed a good local foreman and at Wardour he was lucky to find Richard Cresswell, 'that careful and honest man who will never leave a stone unturned to obey my orders'.[5] Woods' plan for Wardour Park is dated 1764 and shows the site for the new mansion in roughly its present position. There are to be two enormous lakes, one stretching from the old castle to the new house and the other from the new house to South Hill; a greenhouse, an Ionic temple and rotundas in Lady Grove; a magnificent two mile drive across the park from the Shaftesbury road to the mansion; a grotto at the edge of South Hill; a Gothic belvedere also on South Hill and in various other places, a Palladian bridge, a Chinese temple, a Cold Bath and an ice house.[6]

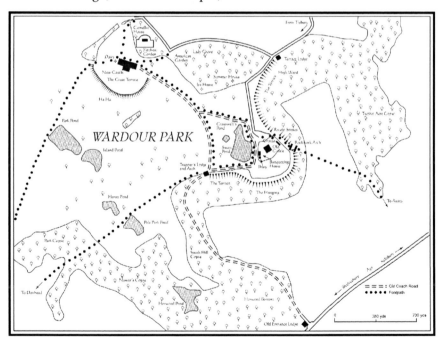

The landscaped park at Wardour laid out for the 8th Lord by Richard Woods in the 1760s and 1770s.

Inevitably, Wood's proposals were not carried out in their entirety. There was the problem of Henry's well-known procrastination. In many letters, Woods expresses exasperation as he explains that 'nothing more is required to inable Rd. Woods to act with a proper Athauthity but only Lord Arundell to <u>sign</u> this paper.' More serious was the problem of payment. There are many urgent requests to get 'cash into the Bankers hands . . . . . . as soon as your Lordship please, after the receipt of this.' Apparently Lord Arundell sometimes complained that Woods was expensive but Woods replied,

> what makes it so, my Lord, is the multiplicity of Business I've always had to settle each time, which generally keep me 9 or 10 days or sometimes more . . . Nevertheless as your Lordship has been a very good Imployer and friend I have no objection to make my next journey easy to you, not that I will take a guinea a day but will make you a present of the visit only allowing the expenses of the road.

View from the south windows of the new castle in 2010, across the ha-ha towards Nowers Copse in the distance.

It is now very difficult to follow the progress of work in Wardour Park from the surviving papers but it is likely that it was undertaken in this order:

1764 improvements in Lady Grove

1765 the Terrace, the ice house, the new coach road

1766 the pond and cascade,

the Cold Bath, the new Terrace or 'Shais road'

1768   the Gothic temple, a cascade

1769   the greenhouse, pineries and heated garden walls

Would it have been better if Brown and not Woods had been employed at Wardour? Probably. Woods' landscapes are small in scale, full of clumps of trees and groves. He failed to achieve the spectacular sweeping landscapes that are the hallmark of Brown. The one was master of 1,000 acres, the other was happier with 100. Brown was a great artist; Woods was a good gardener.

Let us imagine a visit to the park at the end of Henry's life in 1808. We start from the new turnpike road laid out between Wilton and Shaftesbury in 1788. The drive goes through Cock

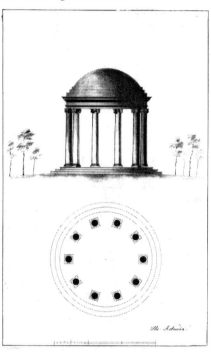

Plan of a rotunda for South Hill, one of many buildings proposed by Woods but never carried out.

Crow Copse (it is now privately owned) and passes for a mile through woods of 'spruce and Scotch fir'. At the point where the drive turns around South Hill, there is a spectacular view across the park towards the new mansion on the left and the ruined old castle on the right. Then the Terrace begins.[7] This mile-long path runs along the side of the great amphitheatre of hills behind the old castle and was made by Woods, perhaps in imitation of the one he had seen at Rievaulx Abbey in Yorkshire. As we walk along the Terrace there are openings in the trees, described in an 1801 Guidebook[8] as,

The old castle as a romantic ruin in the Wardour landscape after a sketch by P. Crocker in the 1820s

happy openings to let in occasionally distant country – Somersetshire and Wiltshire hills, Glastonbury Tor, Stourhead and the magnificent objects in its more immediate neighbourhood, the new stupendous, nondescript structure of Mr. Beckford[9] and the modern mansion of Wardour.

Many visitors continue to the end of the Terrace but we take a narrow path on the left just before the Terrace goes over the rockwork arch. This path leads to the old ruined castle, clad with ivy, where tea is served in the Banqueting House. How lucky Henry is to have a genuine medieval ruin in his park and not to have to build a new one. His family must be long established here. But first we pass a grotto, the work of Josiah Lane of Tisbury, in 1792 and made from brick, sarsen stones and tufa. Josiah and his father have built many famous grottoes, at Painshill, Fonthill and Bowood, all designed to provide a place for contemplation and melancholy. Woods proposed siting the grotto near Horwood Pond and we do not know the reason for this change of site.

We walk across the lawn and make our way to the Banqueting House, 'most nobly kept up for the use of the public who have free admission to the grounds at all times and who here find a large well-furnished room in which to take their refreshments and a person to wait upon them.' There are two other sites to visit – the stone circle and the privy. The circle is in the bushes near the grotto and consists of stones from a prehistoric circle in Tisbury, placed here so that visitors can reflect on the passing of time.[10] The privy is a magnificent three-seater construction where total strangers can sit and engage in conversation while performing this most necessary of activities.

Leaving the old castle, we take the drive across the park, with Swan Pond on the left and Lady Grove on the right. The Grove is a place for quiet walks and solitude. There were plans for various buildings to be placed here, including a large aviary, but in the end Woods built only a Gothic temple[11] and an ice house. The temple is octagonal in shape with three ogee arches open to the south and the total cost was £46. The ice house[12] is an essential requirement for any mansion in which iced wine and desserts are served to visitors. This example has two doors facing north and excellent drainage. Damp was a greater hazard to the ice than heat.

There is one other building to visit on our way across the park, the Cold Bath,[13] between Swan and Cresswell Ponds. This is a luxury item in the repertoire of any country house owner and it became very fashionable in the 18th century. The building consists of a changing room with much needed fireplace and leading off it a plunge bath ten feet by eight feet by five feet deep, with steps leading down. The purpose of the bath is purely medicinal. It is believed that a plunge into cold water will 'chill the nerves, compress the juices, invigorate the spirits and stimulate the digestion.'[14]

We are now approaching the new mansion but must first visit the three acre Kitchen Garden, Woods' most expensive project at Wardour. It cost £1,041 for brick walls, a greenhouse (later called the Camellia

Plan of the Cold Bath built between Swan and Cresswell's Ponds by Richard Woods in 1766.

House) and two pineries. Work began in 1769 and in February 1770 Woods bought 60 orange trees in London for Lord Arundell and planted them here. The pineries are essential for the growing of pineapples, regarded as the greatest delicacy on an aristocratic table. So rare are they that some accounts tell of a landowner renting his best

The Cold Bath portico in 2010, attached to the side of Ark Farm which incorporates the Cold Bath.

pineapples to a neighbour simply as decoration for his table. The plants need a temperature of 70° in order to bear fruit in May and June and this is provided by the heated walls and beds of bark and dung which produce a moist, steamy heat. Each plant fruits only once so succession houses provide new plants from suckers or crowns.

However, Wardour's main horticultural claim to fame is the Camellia House. The first camellias were brought to England from China in 1739 by the Jesuits and were knows as Chinese roses. They are highly prized. The variety at Wardour is the pure white Alba Plena, introduced from China in 1792 by the Slater brothers. Lord Arundell has obtained one of the first specimens.[15]

The north front of the new mansion depicted by P. Crocker in the 1820s.

At last the great mansion looms ahead, a vast compact Palladian villa with its insignificant front door and two projecting wings containing kitchens on the east side and the chapel on the west. This indeed is a family making an enduring statement about social and economic and political power. Before we go inside we must learn about the architects.

First, James Paine, born in 1717 in Hampshire, the son of a carpenter. He became a friend of the great Earl of Burlington and promoted the designs of Andreo Palladio, the 16th century Venetian architect. Paine's

Reynolds' portrait of James Paine and his son in 1764, five years before the father began work on his plans for the new mansion at Wardour. The painting was criticised because the artist shows the father dressed for winter but the son for summer. (Ashmolean Museum, University of Oxford)

hallmark is a compact Palladian villa with a central top-lit staircase and symmetrical pavilion wings. Wardour is his masterpiece. The arrangement of rooms reflects the need for them to be used for entertainment, all running into one another around a central staircase rather than in a straight line as in older houses. Although the rooms are sparsely decorated, the Music Room is an exception with its foliage scrolls on the ceiling and in the centre a copy of Reni's Aurora by Batoni. But Wardour's reputation as a great building rests on the breathtaking staircase hall, described as 'the most glorious Georgian interior of Wiltshire.'[16] It is 60 feet high, curving staircases fly on either side and tall Corinthian columns surround a magnificent gallery.

Paine made an agreement with Lord Arundell on 24 September 1770 for 'Erecting and Building a Capital Mansion House with proper offices thereto'[17] and undertook to provide all the working drawings and visit the site twice a year to review progress. Henry was left to supervise the construction himself and this may have been where a great deal of money was lost. His Clerk of Works was James Brown and the house was finished in 1776. It has 150 windows and over 70 rooms.

The second architect who worked at Wardour was John Soane, born in 1753, son of a bricklayer. He began his career as apprentice to a London architect and studied at the Royal Academy. He had just been appointed architect to the Bank of England in 1788 when Henry

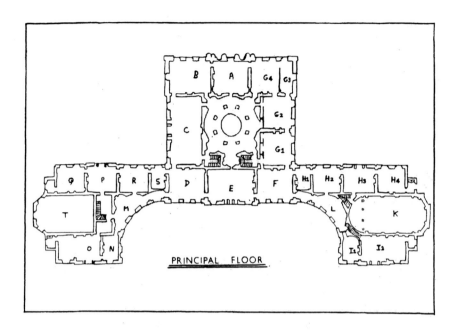

PRINCIPAL FLOOR

PAINE'S PLAN, 1776		AS USED IN 1935	PAINE'S PLAN, 1776		AS USED IN 1935
A	Ante Chamber	Music Room	H4	Suite of Apartments	Lady Arundell's Bedroom
B	Drawing Room	Drawing Room	I1	" "	Chintz Dressing Room
C	Salon	Great Dining Room	I2	" "	Chintz Bedroom
D	Common Dining Room	Blue Drawing Room	K	Upper Chapel	Upper Chapel
E	Great Dining Room	Saloon	L	Ante Chamber	Gallery
F	Library	Library	M	Ante Chamber	Gallery
G1	Suite of Apartments	Boudoir	N	Dressing Room	North Dressing Room
G2	" "	State Bedroom	O	Bedchamber	North Bedroom
G3	" "	Lavatory	P	Breakfast Room	Sitting Room
G4	" "	Little Drawing Room	Q	His Lordship's Room	Bedroom
H1	Suite of Apartments	Bathroom	R	Her Ladyship's Room	Buff Bedroom
H2	" "	Bedroom	S	Book Room	Buff Dressing Room
H3	" "	Ante Room	T	Upper Kitchen	Upper Kitchen

Above the rooms in the main block were six bedrooms and four dressing rooms; and above those, nineteen rooms in the attic for servants.

Paine's plan for the principal floor at the new mansion with the use of rooms in 1935 alongside. Wardour Castle is regarded as Paine's masterpiece.

The main staircase at Wardour Castle, described by Nikolaus Pevsner as 'the most glorious Georgian interior of Wiltshire'.

employed him to enlarge the chapel. Paine designed a top-lit hall as a chapel, between the bedrooms and laundry in the west wing because the law forbade the building of a free-standing Catholic chapel. Henry decided that this was not large enough so in the late 1780s he called in John Soane to enlarge the space with a new sanctuary end. Soane visited Wardour in April 1788 and the work was completed by March 1790. Soane's work at Wardour is generally regarded as a brilliant example of his clever handling of space and light. He extended the sanctuary westwards and built low, galleried wings on each side with a large window set in the curving wall behind the altar.

Two other names are forever associated with the creation of Wardour – Father John Thorpe and Giacomo Quarenghi, architect to the Russian Imperial Court. Thorpe was born in Yorkshire in 1726, educated at St. Omers, joined the Jesuit order and then taught at St. Omers in the 1750s when Henry was one of his pupils. He moved to Rome in 1756 where he became representative for the English Jesuits. His great hobby and consuming interest was collecting works of art and he advised Henry on purchases and despatched for him, at least twice a year, packing cases of pictures and statues from Leghorn to London. He wrote frequently to Henry from 1768 to 1791 and hundreds of his letters survive in the family archives.[18] A few extracts from these letters indicate their close relationship and the problems of supplying a dilatory English peer with exactly the items he wanted for his new mansion:

> August 1769: condolences on the death of the Dowager Lady Arundell but Lord Arundell will have an increased fortune, . . . Prince Altieri will not allow his Claudes to be copied.
>
> March 1770: the purchase is completed of a copy of Raphael's Holy family by Andrea del Sarto.
>
> June 1770: apologies but there is great difficulty of getting any reputable painter to paint drapery over the naked figures of the Sacred Infant and St. John the Baptist, 'in order to satisfy Lord Arundell's prudery'.[19]
>
> November 1770: a promise to purchase scenes from Sacred History, having always 'a strict regard to decency'.

February 1771: the Duke of Dorset, Mr. Constable and Lord Bute are busy making purchases.

April 1771: can obtain a copy of Guido's Aurora with 'their nudities decently covered according to instructions'.[20]

August 1771: purchase of silver and a fine cabinet for Wardour; prayers on the death of Lord Arundell's daughter Anna Maria.

February 1773: Abbé Butler is making strong efforts to legalise the marriage of priests. Chapel plans are proceeding.

March 1773: Batoni has agreed to paint a picture of Agar, her son and the Angel for Lord Arundell.

August 1773: a copy of Cardinal Pole's picture at the Barberini Palace has been made for Wardour; 'there is difficulty getting permission to copy the Pamphili Claudes so I have bribed the Keeper of the Gallery to allow an artist in early in the morning while the family are still in bed.'

December 1774: work on the altar has begun, designed by Quarenghi and to be made of porphyry, agate, rich marbles and pietra dura

September 1775: bought Pieta by Guido Reni for Lord Arundell; also sending pickled tunny-fish, a recipe for ice cream and Cardinal Pole's portrait.

July 1776: the altar is ready and packed and the cost will be more than the estimate – 600 gns. It was carved at Vinelli's masons yard and attracted big crowds.

October 1783: many works of art bound for Wardour have been lost in a shipwreck off the coast of Spain.

June 1778: many books for Wardour have been saved from another shipwreck; sending an inlaid marble table.

Thorpe was an enthusiastic and sensitive supporter of all Henry's schemes to make Wardour chapel the most beautiful Catholic Church in England. He considered proposals for the altar from the Scottish architect James Byres, then living in Rome, but he rejected them and wrote to Henry in 1771: 'Angels holding candlesticks or crucifixes may look pretty in a drawing yet if executed on an altar will perhaps have too much of the Puppet show in England.' Instead, Thorpe chose Giacomo Quarenghi in 1774. He was then aged 30 and gaining a reputation as an artist and architect. A few years later he left Italy for St. Petersburg and remained there for over twenty years building palaces for Catherine the Great as her Court architect. His altar at Wardour is solid and severe with a miniature domed temple on the top.

Thorpe continued to be involved with the Chapel until the end of his life. He provided the design for sanctuary lamps by Luigi Valadier, for the candlesticks, and he sent a carved panel in 1789 showing the Virgin and Child by Monnot. One of the visitors to Wardour during Henry's lifetime, Richard Warner of Bath, recorded his impressions in 1801:[21]

> the chapel displays superlative taste and magnificence ... The tamest fancy must be roused by such a scene and the coolest heart warmed ... it is but proper to add that the attendance of strangers at their services in Wardour Chapel is considered as a compliment and every convenience is provided for their accommodation.

The new mansion was open to the public from the beginning. Visitors were welcomed every day after 12 o'clock and a guide was

A rainwater head on the new castle, showing the date of completion of the building.

provided. If they were lucky they would hear Lady Arundell singing in the Music Room as they ascended the stairs. All the apartments were richly furnished and hung with costly paintings. The state bedroom contained an ornate bed which had been slept in by three Kings: Charles I, Charles II and James II. John

Britton who published his *Beauties of Wiltshire* in 1801 commented that there were 26 rooms on show and warned,

the embellishments of this mansion (speaking generally), appear to be associated with ideas of religion – monks curiously carved in ivory, crucifixes elegantly wrought, paintings of Saints and martyrs, both male and female, holy families, resurrections and ascensions . . .

The Music Room with portraits of Lady Blanche and the 8th Lord. The picture on the ceiling is a copy of Reni's Aurora by Batoni.

Visitors were taken up the grand staircase to the Saloon, the most important room, hung with the best pictures and thence around the state rooms and to the chapel. Some visitors commented that the house was not remarkable for the magnificence of its furniture but the paintings were outstanding. There were, of course, many family portraits on the walls including the four paintings by Reynolds of the 7th and 8th Lords and their wives; also four Popes, six cardinals, ten Christs, six Marys and three Holy families. It is impossible to know how many of the paintings were originals and how many were copies produced by Father Thorpe. The following is a small selection from the list compiled by the 10th Lord in the 1820s for Colt Hoare's *History of Modern Wiltshire*:

The drawing room with the famous Chippendale satinwood cabinet, photographed for Country Life *in 1930.*

Two Sea Views, a Calm and a Storm, Vernet

Tobit Going to Meet His Son, G. Douw

A Shepherd Boy Playing on Bagpipes, Caravaggio

St. Bernardine of Siena, Titian

A Groom and a White Horse, Rembrandt

An Old Woman Looking at a Piece of Money, Rubens

A Child of the Medici Family, Titian

Hugo Grotius, Rubens

An Old Woman Peeling Apples, Tenier

Jacob's Departure from Canaan, N. Poussin

Joseph in Prison, Murillo

Sir Thomas More, Holbein

Agar in the Wilderness, Batoni

Joshua Reynolds' receipt for payment for his portrait of Lady Arundell. The picture is now in the San Antonio Museum of Art, Texas.

It would be an interesting enquiry to find out where these paintings are now.[22] Many are in American galleries.

Finally, we ought to meet some of the dozens of men who worked on the building and the landscape of Wardour to produce the magnificence of which Henry was so proud. They are all silent. They have left us nothing of their thoughts and feelings as they toiled through cold winters and wet summers to create what we still enjoy today. We know only a few names but they must represent all those who laboured to create this great work:

Mr Turner ye Plummer

Jackson the slates

Lake the brickmaker

Hannah Shepherd (for weeding before
the House, 4s . 6d a week)

Richard Martin ye Carpenter (9s. 0d a
week)

Mr Blockley the locksmith

Edwards the glazier (6s. 0d a week)

John Singleton ye well digger

William Clark, gardener (9s. 7d a week)

Noah Singleton ye lime burner

Thomas King, bricklayer (5s. 4d a
week)

John Hawkins ye carter

ye Ratt catcher . . .

A window on the south front of the castle, looking into the Music Room.

10

'Trying to Pay Grandfather's Bills'

JAMES Everard, Henry's eldest grandson by his eldest daughter Maria Christina, became the 10th Lord Arundell in July 1817. His mother, who inherited the estates, had married her first cousin, Henry's closest heir to the title and thus the inheritance of estates and title proceeded together.

James Everard should have been the saviour of Wardour. Most estates, encumbered by vast debts, survived because of the succession of an heir who was parsimonious, careful and cautious. Instead, James's attempts to pay his grandfather's bills ended in disaster. He himself became bankrupt, he was hounded by creditors and went to live in Rome where he died in June 1834. Admittedly, the challenge was enormous. His grandfather left an estate drastically reduced from its original size and when he died in 1808 the trustees were still struggling to identify his debts. Selling land meant that the remaining estate could never be large enough to produce an income sufficient to maintain an enormous mansion and a role for the family in public life. Henry had been a disaster and he cast a long shadow.

There was no shortage of advice from fellow-sufferers about what an impoverished aristocrat like James should do when he inherited. First, he should check his accounts frequently and not rely on others to do it. Lady Stafford, wife of the 1st Marquess of Stafford, wrote to her sons in July 1794:

The 10th Lord as the scholar and collaborator of Sir Richard Colt Hoare in his History of Wiltshire, published in the 1820s and 1830s.

To be quite free of debt every quarter, look into your own Bills. This is the method most certain not to be cheated, nor not to spend more than your Income . . . every Man should know the state of his own affairs . . . what he has to spend and how he spends it. Till your father adopted this Method (even with his large Income) he was continually distress'd for want of Money and now he has plenty to spare.[1]

In contrast, James does not appear to have taken any interest in accounts and he delegated the task to his lawyers who knew little about such matters.

Although James probably never knew him, there was a young man in London at this time making a colossal fortune by adopting the very methods that would have served the Arundells well. He was James Morrison and he became so wealthy that he bought the neighbouring estate of Fonthill in 1829 and died the richest commoner in Britain.[2] His success in his wholesale haberdasher's business had come about due to his meticulous attention to accounts and his daily involvement with his business, but for an aristocrat to learn from 'trade' would have been unthinkable.

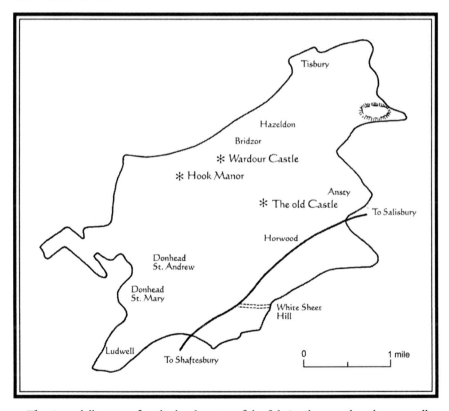

The Arundell estate after the bankruptcy of the 8th Lord was reduced to a small area around Wardour.

Besides his vast debts, James Everard inherited his grandfather's tendency to procrastination.[3] His letters are full of proposals never carried out, schemes considered and then half implemented and decisions delayed. This does not contribute to financial stability. In other ways James was an attractive character; he was a scholar keenly involved with his friend Richard Colt Hoare in producing the *History of Modern Wiltshire*; he was a book collector; he was concerned about the deplorable condition of cottages on the Wardour estate and undertook a modernisation programme; he was a loving and faithful husband. In politics he was less attractive; he was deeply conservative to the extent that he was the only Catholic peer who voted against the Reform Bill in 1832.

A second remedy for aristocratic debt was a simple economy campaign. It was perhaps the greatest challenge for any aristocratic family, accustomed to lavish spending. But it was possible, as witness the 10th Duke of Bedford in the 1830s who struggled to pay his father's enormous debts by insisting on 'prompt payments and short accounts' in the household budget.

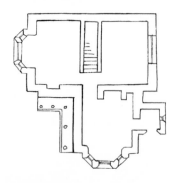

Cemetery Lodge, one of the many cottages built by the 10th Lord at Wardour, in spite of financial problems.

He checked personally all expenditure everyday and insisted on monthly accounts until the strain gave his steward a nervous breakdown and he changed to quarterly accounting. He even insisted on the re-use of half-burnt candles at Woburn, his palatial mansion in Bedfordshire.[4]

James found such a policy impossible to carry out although he considered demolishing Wardour and building a smaller house. Nothing was done, but his improvement schemes – new cottages, new stables, a peach house and planting schemes for the Park and Castle Ditches,

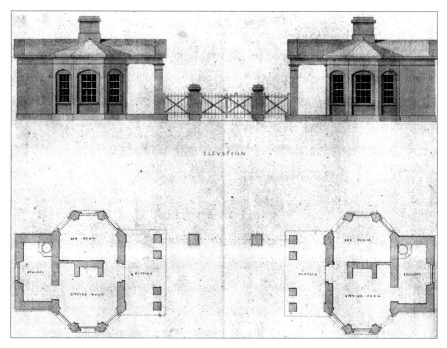

Proposal for new entrance lodges on the new Salisbury to Shaftesbury road; never built.

were not the hall-marks of a miser. His book collecting cannot have been a small expenditure either. When he died in 1834 he left his personal library to his old school, Stonyhurst. The books, for which a special room was later built, included the first part of Froissart's Chronicles and a First Folio of Shakespeare. They are now so valuable that they are kept in a special high security location. Also in the legacy was a large collection of Albrecht Dürer engravings and a bundle of medieval, illuminated manuscripts.[5]

A third remedy was the expedient of living abroad in exile. Lord Curzon's grandmother recommended this strategy to her family and

The Arundell Library at Stonyhurst College, built to house the magnificent library given to the college by the 10th Lord.

remarked, 'there is great advantage in getting the Water between a man and his embarrassments.'[6] This removed the individual from the threat of law suits and prison sentences but unless it was accompanied by rigorous economy it was no solution. James escaped abroad in 1826 for a few months (having offered his creditors a settlement of 10 shillings in the pound) but returned in 1827 for a short time and then went to live permanently in Rome. One result of his absence was to leave his affairs and estates too much in the hands of lawyers (Messers Chitty and Bowles in Shaftesbury) who, whatever their financial skill, were not interested in estate management and improvement.

Another, oft discussed remedy for debt was the 'good marriage'. If an heiress could be enticed to join the family, there might be financial benefits for generations to come. Unfortunately James made a marriage which was financially unproductive even if it was personally happy.

In February 1811 at the age of 25, he married Lady Mary Grenville at Buckingham House, her family home in Pall Mall.

On the surface, this was simply a marriage with the daughter of a wealthy and illustrious family. Mary's grandfather had been Prime Minister from 1763 to 1765 and is best remembered as the man who imposed the Stamp Tax on the American colonies. Mary's father, the 1st Marquess of Buckingham, converted Stowe, the family home into a palace and sulked for 23 years because George III refused to make him a Duke. Gillray drew cartoons of him as an overgrown pig with his snout in the public trough.[7] Mary's uncle, William Grenville, was Prime Minister from 1806 to 1807, a great ally of Charles James Fox and with him promoted Catholic emancipation.[8] Another uncle, Thomas, was a passionate book collector and may have influenced James in that hobby.[9]

So far so good, but Mary's generation and the next were a different story. Mary's brother Richard was immensely fat, greedy and ambitious. He advised James Everard on his financial affairs. There could have been no one less qualified to give such advice. He expected to be given high political office in 1806, when his uncle was Prime Minister, but he was made only President of the Board of Trade.[10] His personal financial mismanagement was so serious that in 1833 his estates at Stowe were handed over to trustees and he went to live abroad. However, this was not effective as he bought a yacht with specially widened gangways to accommodate his enormous girth and used it as a floating palace to travel round Europe. The trustees all resigned in 1836, protesting that their job was impossible. In the same year he returned to live at Stowe where his steward had invented a lifting machine to convey him from one floor to another. Unfortunately, the steward died from a broken neck when he fell through the lift hole so the device was abandoned and the Duke was confined to one floor. He had been made Duke of Buckingham in 1822 as a reward for supporting Lord Liverpool, the Prime Minister but that did not prevent him from leaving a colossal debt when he died in 1839. James gained no financial benefit from his marriage into this profligate family.

A final remedy for debt was that the head of the family should find some lucrative employment. The Arundells had never been able to benefit from the holding of public office because of their Catholic faith but by the 1820s the Penal Laws were seldom enforced and some public employment might have been possible. In 1827 James reported from Paris that Lord Lansdowne, the Home Secretary was about to offer him a post but nothing came of it.

The most beneficial action that James could have taken was to improve and exploit his remaining estate. But the hereditary principle and a flair for entrepreneurship do not often coincide. In James's case they were a million miles apart. He still owned 6,000 fertile, agricultural acres in Wiltshire which could produce a good income. The first requirement was to appoint a steward whose responsibility was the estate's development. James failed to do this and continued to use his solicitors in Shaftesbury as agents and accountants. They may have been legally astute but they knew nothing about improving the productivity of the land. In any case, they were preoccupied with fending off creditors. Wardour needed a land steward like Francis Blackie[11] who worked for Coke of Norfolk from 1816 to 1832 and ran the estate as an efficient business enterprise. Not until John Jeffrey of Shaftesbury was appointed estate agent by the 11th Lord in the 1840s did the Wardour estate have anything like modern management. The meticulous estate survey books of 1851 are testimony to his skill. He discovered that more than £2,000 of annual income had been 'lost' each year due to lax accounting.[12]

James and his wife took up residence in Wardour Castle in 1814, three years before his father died. There are many bundles of his letters and papers in the family archives, until recently tied with the string and quill pens in use at the time. The following examples give a brief glimpse of his troubles and attempts to solve them. First a letter from his bankers:[13]

36 Pall Mall, 18 April 1816

My Dear Sir,

I do not know whether you are aware of the extent to which your account with us is overdrawn being now £1,370, besides the Note of hand for £400. My Partners beg that you may be requested to suspend all further Drafts till measures can be taken to set your account right, to which they solicit your early attention . . . overdrawn accounts are particularly disadvantageous to Bankers. We wish to avoid them whenever it is possible . . .

I have the honour to be

Dear Sir

your faithful and obedient and humble servant

S. Bernard Morland

A few months later there was a letter from James's uncle, Lord Clifford, one of the Wardour trustees, complaining that his father the 9th Lord had requested £10,000 for the marriage of his daughter to Sir John Talbot but this could not be paid. Then a note requesting money to settle accounts from Messers Coutts & Co. in London and on 16 November 1819 a summons to Lord Arundell to appear in Court where Benjamin Merriman claimed payment of debts. A note on the summons reminds James that as a Peer he is privileged from arrest, (the same escape route that his grandfather had used two decades earlier and which continued to let peers off the hook until 1948). We do not know the outcome of the case but he was summoned again on 5 May 1820 for debts owed to James Henderson. Again the result is not recorded.

On 7 October 1820 came a desperate plea for payment from John Cook, one of the Arundell tenants at Irnham, to Mr. Chitty in Shaftesbury:[14]

Dear Sir,

Several months having elapsed since I heard from you, I am induced once more to address you in the hope that you are by this time enabled to let me have the money due to my Father. Unwilling as I am to be troublesome to you on this subject, necessity compels me to earnestly solicit payment. My journey to London last May was principally for that purpose and my disappointment was very great when I found I could not obtain it, even after the sacrifice I had made. I know not in what other terms to ask for it with civility but as an inducement to your exertions to procure me the money, I will make you a present of ten pounds provided the sum due is paid within one month from the date of this letter.

I remain Sir

Your obedient Servant

John Cook

This deferential letter appears to have had no result.

The courts were again involved. In 1820 Chancery settled on payment of Arundell debts at 17 shillings in the pound but this was reduced to 13s. 4d. in the pound a few years later, because the money could not be found, and then to 10 shillings. James was in despair. He wrote in 1823 that he was doing his best but 'I am determined to starve in a cottage in Wiltshire if I am to starve anywhere.'[15] Two years later he decided to leave Wardour for ever and informed Mr Chitty in Shaftesbury:

My determination is to quit this place by the 1st September, probably for ever . . . I shall be happy when I have got away from this place. I shall be quiet . . . my only difficulty will be how to find the means to go. When I am gone I can live on a little and that, with tranquillity, will be better than the splendid misery I have been forced to endure for some years . . . Pray suggest some ideas about letting this House.[16]

The possibility of letting Wardour Castle to a rich tenant then became a constant concern. In August 1826, James wrote to Mr. Chitty saying that he hoped Lord Grosvenor[17] had not given up all thoughts of residing at Wardour. Such a tenant would be ideal and give the whole family peace of mind. Lord Grosvenor could name his own terms and the sacristan would look after the chapel which would be quite separate.

Unfortunately the Grosvenors did not rent the mansion and the problem was unresolved when James and his wife left Southampton for the continent in September 1826. They settled in Rouen and from there James wrote, with great satisfaction, to tell Mr. Chitty that £100 had lasted him a whole month and he would try to make the next £100 last two months 'if I do not go to Paris.' And then a memorable example of class pride:

> I have received a letter from you containing a proposal to let Wardour to Mr. Mortimer[18] – I cannot accede to it. I am humbled but not so low as to put a Scotch weaver in my House, sooner shall it fall piecemeal to ruin. Sir Joseph Radcliffe's Scotch servants were dirty enough. Mr. Mortimer's will be a bad edition of his.

James made a brief visit to London and Wardour in May 1827. He decided to sell Place Farm in Tisbury.[19] 'What am I to do? Do consider how little I have lived upon and what it is to lose my credit . . . I must discharge my servants and live in a garret.'[20] He returned to Paris as quickly as possible and then went on to Rome. Reports from the agent in Shaftesbury described for him the problems suffered by workmen and servants at Wardour because they were owed so much money. The long, cold winter of 1827 was 'distressing, with many on the Parish'. The price of corn reached record levels and families were on the verge of starvation. Mr. Baker the inn keeper at Wardour complained that he had to turn away customers because 'the House is not allowed to be shown.'[21]

By June 1828 James and his wife were well settled in Rome, having 'nearly made up my mind to stay here for life and never to go to Wardour again.'[22] He was lucky to be out of the country when a Mr. Phelips brought an action against him in the King's Bench. In fact, Lord Arundell was pursued by creditors until the day he died in Rome, in June 1834. His wife was grief-stricken but commented to friends that at last she would be able to buy a bottle of wine without three days' discussion. His brother Henry took up residence at Wardour in 1831 and for 30 years gave the estate a calm and careful management. He also filled the castle with the sound of children for the first time for many years.

11

'A Wild, Roving, Vagabond Life'

ONE day in August 1851[1] a young, aristocratic Englishwoman was walking with her sister on the Ramparts in Boulogne. She noticed a man walking towards them. 'He was five feet eleven inches in height, very broad, thin and muscular; he had dark hair, black, clearly defined, sagacious eyebrows, a brown weather-beaten complexion . . . ' When he had passed she turned to her sister and whispered, 'That man will marry me.' She was Isabel Arundell, daughter of the 11th Lord's cousin, Henry. He was Richard Burton, later to be one of the most famous and controversial Victorian explorers and writers, the subject of over a dozen biographies.

Next day they walked on the Ramparts again. He followed them and before they turned, he chalked on a wall, 'May I speak to you?' Isabel chalked in reply, 'No, mother will be angry.' and they both returned home. However, some days later an older mutual friend introduced them and they spoke for a few minutes. And again a few days later. Isabel was almost overcome. 'I used to turn red and pale, hot and cold, dizzy and faint, sick and trembling and my knees nearly gave way under me . . . .' Her mother noticed the symptoms and sent for a doctor who prescribed pills. Isabel put them in the fire.

Some weeks later, a cousin organised a dance and made sure that Richard Burton was invited: 'That was a Night of nights; he waltzed with me once and spoke to me several times. I kept my sash where he put his arm around my waist to waltz, and my gloves. I never wore them again.' And that was it. No more contact for five years. Richard set out on expeditions to Asia and Africa.

Isabel's father, Henry Arundell, grew up at Wardour and was given a wing of the castle as his home when he first married in 1827. Although he moved to London and worked discreetly as a wine merchant after his second marriage and the birth of his eleven children, the whole family made frequent visits to Wardour. Isabel was born on 20 March 1831 and was known as Puss from her habit of always being inquisitive. She was considered beautiful except for a heavy jaw.

In August 1856, Isabel and her sister Blanche were walking in the Botanical Gardens in London. They suddenly noticed Richard Burton. They stopped and shook hands. Next day they met again and spoke for longer and every day for the next fortnight. Isabel remembered she trod on air. Then suddenly Richard asked her if she could give up her family and the life she led and live the life that Lady Hester Stanhope,[2] the famous early nineteenth traveller, had lived in Damascus. She replied,

> I don't want to think it over, I have been thinking about it for five years, ever since I first saw you at Boulogne. I have prayed for you every day, morning and night; I have followed all your career minutely, I have read every word you ever wrote and I would rather have a crust and a tent with you than be Queen of all the world. And I say now, Yes, Yes, YES.

Then he said, 'Your people will not give you to me.' Isabel answered, 'I know that but I belong to myself. I give myself away.'

Nothing more happened because Richard was planning an expedition to Africa. They agreed to write to one another but for that to be possible Richard had to be 'known' to her family. He therefore called at 14 Montagu Place, the Arundell family home and they play acted that they had never met before. Their last real meeting was on 3 October 1856 in

Sir Richard Burton as he was known to the public; the spear wound on his cheek which he suffered in 1855 in east Africa, is clearly shown. (National Portrait Gallery, London)

Hyde Park. Isabel put around Richard's neck a medal of the Virgin Mary on a steel chain. A few days later he wrote her a note saying goodbye and thereafter she wore it in a little bag on a chain around her neck.

During the next three years, Isabel wrote to Richard twice a month but letters from him were few and far between. There was one gap of twenty months in letters from him. On 21 May 1859 he arrived in London. They met in a friend's house. 'For an instant we both stood dazed . . . . . . we rushed into each other's arms. I cannot attempt to describe the joy of that moment.' Isabel went home and told her mother Richard Burton had proposed. Her mother replied that Burton was the only man she would never allow her daughter to marry. She would rather see Isabel in her coffin. No compromise was possible. That summer the whole family went to live at Wardour Castle and Isabel considered her next move.

Who was Richard Burton? Why was he so unsuitable? He was the son of an army officer, born on 19 March 1821. He spent his childhood in France and Italy and entered Trinity College, Oxford in 1840 but was expelled for wild behaviour. His father wanted him to train as a priest but Richard chose the army and his father bought him a commission in the Indian army for £500. He arrived in Bombay in 1842 and was sent to work for General Sir Charles Napier who had conquered the province of Sind. Richard had a gift for languages and an extraordinary ability to enter into local people's lives. He often wore native clothes. He and T.E. Lawrence would make an interesting comparison. One of his more unusual assignments was to investigate the male brothels of Karachi. His report led to their suppression but he made enemies and was sent home in 1849 on extended leave. He began to write about his experiences in India and quickly produced four books.[3] It was at this point that he first met Isabel in Boulogne.

In April 1853 he decided to leave the world of books and make an expedition in disguise to Medina and Mecca, the holy places of Islam. Less than half a dozen Europeans had ever visited those shrines. He made preparations in Cairo, changed his identify to Sheikh Abdullah, a medicine man, had himself circumcised and set off on the pilgrim boat to Yanbu. He reached Mecca on 11 September and performed all the customary ceremonies. He made detailed notes, which later became the material for three books about his experiences.

Then in October 1854, he led an expedition to Somalia, aiming to visit Harar, a town in the interior, which had never been visited by a European. The expedition was not a success nor was a second attempt in the following year when Burton was wounded on his left cheek by a spear which left a scar for the rest of his life.[4] He eventually returned to London in 1856 and met Isabel in the Botanical Gardens.

Richard Burton dressed as Sheikh Abdullah for his secret journey to Mecca in 1853.

Burton's next ambition was to return to Africa and solve the mystery of the source of the Nile,[5] leading an expedition organised by the Royal Geographical Society. He was given two more years leave from the East India Company (surely in total the longest leave in history) and set out for Africa in December 1856 with John Hanning Speke,[6] another Indian army officer. This expedition has been the subject of countless books, essays and films.[7] It lasted two years and included the discovery of Lake Tanganyika, which Burton claimed as the source of the Nile, Speke's discovery of Lake Victoria and his assertion (correctly) that this was the source of the Nile and their subsequent quarrel over who was correct.

Burton returned to London in May 1859. There were lectures, reports and the inevitable books to write about the lakes of Central Africa. The controversy over the Nile rumbled on. Burton had made a great name for himself, whoever was correct. This then was the man Isabel wanted to marry; not exactly the sort of man to be happy with a house in London and a weekend cottage at Wardour, with plenty of fishing. By October 1859, she decided she had waited long enough and wrote a frank letter to her mother. It must be one of the most memorable letters ever to pass between a daughter and her mother and is worth quoting at length:

October 1859

My Dearest Mother,

I feel quite grateful to you for inviting my confidence. It is the first time you have ever done so and the occasion shall not be neglected. It will be a great comfort to me to tell you all . . . I feel nothing in common with the world I live in. I dreamt of a Companion and a Life that would suit me exactly, and I them. Like many other people, I suppose, I found my heart yearning and my tastes developing towards quite opposite things to those which fall naturally in my way. I am rather ashamed to tell you that I fell in love with Captain Burton at Boulogne, and would have married him at any time between this and then, if he had asked me. The moment I saw his brigand-daredevil look, I set him up as an idol, determined that he was the only man I would marry; but he never knew it until three years ago, before he went to Africa. . .

I want to '*Live*'. I hate the artificial existence in London; I hate the life of a vegetable in the country; I want a wild, roving, vagabond life. I am young, strong and hardy, with good nerves; I like roughing it, and I always want to do something daring and spirited; you will certainly repent it, if you keep me tied up. I wonder that you do not see the magnitude of the position offered to me. His immense talent and adventurous life must command interest. A master-mind like his exercises power and influence over all around him; but I love him because I find in him so much depth of feeling, and a generous heart; because, knowing him to be as brave as a lion, he is yet so gentle, of a delicate, sensitive nature, and the soul of honour.

I love him purely, passionately, and respectfully; there is no void in my heart, it is at rest for ever with him. It is part of my nature, part of myself, the basis of all my actions, part of my religion; my whole soul is absorbed in it. I have given my every feeling to him and kept nothing back for myself or for the world. I would this moment sacrifice and leave *all* to follow his fortunes, even if you all cast me out – if the world tabooed me, and no compensation *could* be given to me for *his* loss. Whatever the world may condemn of lawless or strong opinions, whatever he is to the world, he is perfect to me, and I would not have him otherwise than he is . . .

That is my side of the business, and now I will turn to your few points. You have said that 'you do not know who he is, that you do not meet him anywhere'. I don't like to hear you say the first, because it makes you out illiterate, and you know how clever you are; but as to your not meeting him, considering the particular sort of society which you seek with a view to marrying your daughters, you are not likely to meet him there, because it bores him, and it is quite out of his line. In these matters he is like a noble, simple savage, and has lived too much in the desert to comprehend the snobberies of our little circles in London. He is a world-wide man and his life and talents open every door to him; he is a great man all over the East. In the literary circles in London and in great parties, where you and I would be part of the crowd, he would be remarkable as a star, also amongst scientific men and in the clubs. Most great houses[8] are only too glad to get him. The only two occasions in which he came out last season it was because I begged him to, and he was bored to death. In public life everyone knows him.

As to birth, he is just as good as we are;[9] all his people belong to good old families. The next subject is religion. With regard to this he *appears* to disbelieve, pretends to self-reliance, quizzes good, and fears no evil. He leads a good life, has a natural worship of God, innate honour, and does unknown good. *At present* he is following no form; at least, none that he *owns* to. He says there is nothing between Agnosticism and Catholicity. He wishes to be married in the Catholic Church, says that I must practise my own religion, and that our children must be Catholics, and I give such promise in writing. I myself do not care about people *calling* themselves Catholics, if they are not so in actions, and Captain Burton's life is far more Christian, more gentlemanly, more useful, and more pleasing to God – I am sure – than many who *call* themselves Catholics and whom we know.

No.3 point is money, and here I am before *you*, terribly crestfallen – there is nothing except his pay. As captain, that is, I believe, £600 a year in India, and £300 in England. We want to try and get the Consulship of Damascus, where we could have a life after both our hearts, and where the vulgarity of poverty would not make itself apparent. If you do not disinherit me, I shall settle my portion on him and after, on any children we may have, in which case he would insure his life. He may have expectations or not, but we can't rely on them.

Now, dearest mother, I think we should treat each other fairly. Let him go to my father, and ask for me properly. Knowing you as I do, your ideas and prejudices, I know that a man of different religion and no means, would stand in a disagreeable position; so does he, and I will *not* have him insulted. I don't ask you to approve, nor to like it; I don't expect it. I do entreat your blessing, and even a *passive*, reluctant consent to anything that I may do. We shall never marry anyone else, and never give each other up, should we remain so all our lives. Do not accuse me of deception, because I shall see him and write to him whenever I get a chance, and if you drive me to it I shall marry him in defiance, because he is by far my first object in life, and the day he (if ever) gives me up I will go straight into a convent.

If you could think your Catholic friends and relatives will blame you, shut your eyes, give me no wedding, no trousseau, let me get married how I can; but when it is *done*, acknowledge to yourself that I neither *could* nor *would* be dishonourable enough to marry any other man, that God made no law against *poor* people becoming attached to each other, that I am of an age when you can only advise but not hinder me, that your leave once asked, my duty ends, that your life is three parts run and mine is before me and that if I choose to live out of the 'World' that forms *your* happiness, what is it to you? How does it hurt you? I have got to live with him night and day, all my life. The man you would choose I should loathe. I see all the disadvantages, and am willing to accept them with him. Why should you object? I do not ask you to share it.

Do think it all over in earnest and if you love me as you say you do – and I believe it well – do be generous and kind about this . . . I only wait a kind word from you.

Your fondly attached child

Isabel Arundell

When the reply came it was perhaps no surprise. 'No, No, No, Richard is not a Christian and he has no money.' Isabel eventually decided to act alone. She discussed the problem with her father who said he consented 'if your mother consents.' Her mother refused again and warned that she would suffer permanent paralysis if Isabel persisted. Isabel then visited a family friend, Cardinal Wiseman.[10] He agreed to marry the couple secretly so long as Richard promised to allow Isabel the free practice of her faith and that all children should be brought up as Catholics. On 21 January 1861 Isabel told her parents that she was going to spend a few weeks in the country with friends. The next morning she and Richard were married in the Church of Our Lady of the Assumption in Warwick Street with only six guests.

Isabel and Richard with members of her family on a visit to Wardour in the 1860s.

The honeymoon was spent at Wardour and they returned to London some weeks later. Mrs. Arundell had discovered what had happened. Isabel noted in her diary that paralysis had not afflicted her mother. In fact she received them warmly, explaining that all she had really worried about was that Isabel would not be received in Society. 'We were as happy as it is given to any mortals out of heaven to be,' wrote Isabel in her diary.

In a sense, the next thirty years might seem uneventful in comparison with the dramas of the previous ten. Richard decided that a career in the diplomatic service would provide an opportunity for foreign travel, with leisure to write. Isabel said she was prepared to follow her husband wherever he went, becoming his manager, editor and accountant as well as wife. It was a perfect marriage and Isabel never doubted that she had made the correct decision to elope with Richard. The Foreign Office first appointed him consul at Fernando Po, a small island off the west coast of Africa, too dangerous for Isabel to accompany him and then in September 1864, consul in Santos, Brazil. This time Isabel went too and they travelled all over South America. The best posting, however, was to Damascus in 1869. 'I loved Damascus' wrote Isabel 'my pear, the Garden of Eden, the Promised Land; my beautiful city with her swelling domes and tapering minarets.' They both wore Arab dress and absorbed Arab culture. Isabel wrote the *Inner Life of Syria, Palestine and the Holy Land* which, with her later books on India and Egypt, gave her top position as most prolific Arundell author in the admittedly short list of Arundells as authors.

Unfortunately the Garden of Eden did not last long. There were bitter quarrels with colleagues and in 1872 Richard was posted to Trieste, again as consul. He had hoped for an ambassadorial post but there were advantages in Trieste because it was almost a sinecure and gave the opportunity for research and writing. Isabel was determined to dislike Trieste from the start and she described the post as 'commercial work in a small, civilised European seaport, under-ranked and underpaid.' They eventually settled in great comfort in the twenty roomed Palazzo Gossleth, a Palladian villa near the harbour. Whenever they returned to England they visited Wardour. In 1876 Isabel recorded in her diary, 'went to Wardour where there had been a great storm; some big oaks had been torn up in the pheasant copse near the castle. We came in for an amazing village dance.'

It was at this point that Isabel became hyper-conscious of her status, perhaps to compensate for the lack of recognition given to her husband. She researched the title conferred on the 1st Lord by Emperor Rudolf and began to style herself Countess Arundell when she realised the title passed to all his descendants, female as well as male. She announced that she had discovered Richard was descended from Louis XIV of France. The greatest disappointment was the absence of children. Although Richard had contracted syphilis in India this should not have made him infertile. There are notes in Isabel's papers about remedies for infertility and lists of 'Pills Supposed to Make People Have Children.'[11] But nothing worked.

Many people supposed that Richard's greatest work was all behind him. In fact, the last ten years of his life in the 1880s were the years when he produced the books that made him and Isabel famous, and notorious, and for which they are particularly remembered today. But that probably says more about our obsession with sex than theirs.

If you visit Khajuraho in India today, (one of the main tourist sites with its great Chandela temples, decorated with erotic carvings) you will be offered many translations of the Indian sex manual, the *Kama Sutra*, all fully illustrated; but the most expensive is always the one translated 'from the original by Richard Burton'. [12] Not bad for an author who died 120 years ago. Richard had always been particularly interested in sex since he visited the brothels in Karachi on official duties. In 1863 he helped set up the Anthropological Society of London to discuss human behaviour and fight "respectability" which he loathed. He hated what he called the 'Mrs Grundys of English society'. He and Isabel were frequent visitors to Fryston, the Yorkshire country house of Monkton Miles who kept the largest library of erotica in Britain.

As his duties in Trieste became increasingly part-time, Burton decided in 1883 to begin publication of a series of Indian and Arabic sex manuals. However, in order to avoid prosecution under the 1857 Obscene Publications Act, he and an old colleague from India days, Foster Arbuthnot, set up the Kama Shastri Society. It had only two members and was simply a cover for their publications since the books carried only the Society's name. Books were sold by mail order only and 'for private circulation'. No details were given of the translators or printers. In 1883 they published the *Kama Sutra*, the ancient Sanskrit guide to love making; in 1885 the *Ananga Ranga*, another Sanskrit sex manual; in 1886 *The Tales of the Arabian Nights* in 16 volumes, with all the sexual content included and explicit footnotes; and in 1890 when he died, Burton had just completed the translation of *The Scented Garden*, the

Isabel Burton in later life, when the promotion of Richard's schemes had become her full-time occupation.

famous Arabic sex manual. It was a stupendous achievement. Burton believed it was the summit of his career.

The Arabian Nights was a sensational success. Burton ordered 1,000 copies to be printed and expected to sell 500, if he was lucky. He received orders for 2,000 immediately and pocketed a £16,000 income for an outlay of £6,000. He wrote to a friend, 'I have struggled for 47 years . . . I never had a compliment nor a thank you nor a single farthing. I translate a doubtful book in my old age and I immediately make £10,000. Now that I know the tastes of England, we need never be without money.' Isabel was quite open about her part in the publication of the books. She said she read every word and they had done her no harm.

Predictably, the outcry was loud and long. It was soon discovered in England that Burton had translated the books. 'Burton For The Sewers' concluded the Edinburgh Review. The Echo called *The Arabian Nights*, 'a morally filthy book . . . what might have been acceptable to Asiatic populations ages ago is absolutely unfit for a Christian population now."[13] Richard and Isabel were quite unabashed. He wrote,

> I don't care a button about being prosecuted and if the matter comes to a fight, I will walk into court with my Bible and my Shakespeare and my Rabelais under my arm and prove to them that before they condemn me, they must cut half of <u>them</u> out and not allow them to be circulated in public.

Richard made notes of the arguments he would use in court:

§ My publications will help British people understand more of Islamic and Hindu culture; as rulers of the greatest Muslim and Hindu empire in the world this is essential.

§ I am promoting healthy living because repression and ignorance lead to perversion. 'Mental aphrodisiac excitement' leads to illness.

§ The opposition is despicable – the National Vigilance Association
and the Mrs Grundys are 'a troop of busybodies captained by licensed
blackmailers'.

Perhaps he regretted that the case never came to court.

What was the significance of this last phase of Burton's work? Vast
claims have been made for it: 'he introduced sex to Victorian England',
'he fought for the emotional liberation of the British people'.[14] More
moderately, W.G. Archer believed that Burton's translation of the *Kama
Sutra* began 'our modern understanding of Indian art and culture.'[15]
The Arundell family were certainly proud of the Burtons. Isabel Fagan
remembered their kindness to her father when he was a young man in
London,

> The Burtons took their lonely young nephew under their wing – to
> the opera, music hall and theatre, dining and wining at places far
> beyond his meagre pocket. Woe
> betide anyone who later spoke
> disparagingly of Richard Burton.
> Though viewed with disapproval
> by hypocritical Victorians for his
> unorthodoxy, he nevertheless
> instilled admiration in my father's
> heart.[16]

In 1886 Richard was awarded
a knighthood. He died in Trieste on
29 October 1890 from a heart attack.
Isabel called a priest to give Extreme
Unction claiming that Richard had
moved secretly into the Catholic
Church, a process she claimed he

*Richard Burton working in his
bedroom at Trieste in the 1880s. He
died in this room in October 1890.*

had begun many years earlier in the chapel at Wardour. Eight Masses were said for his soul at churches in Trieste and then, after plaster casts were taken of his head, hands and feet, he was embalmed in a zinc coffin for transport to London. Madame Tussauds displayed a model of him in his Mecca robes and described him as a national hero.

Isabel packed up all their belongings – 8,000 books and 200 boxes of papers and diaries. She decided to burn the two copies of his translation of *The Scented Garden* which he completed the day before he died. This is the event which more than any other has injured her reputation and caused her to be remembered first and foremost as a pyromaniac. The stories of what happened have been greatly exaggerated. There were reports that Isabel burnt all his papers in a conflagration that lasted several days. This version probably owes its origin to Daisy Letchford, Isabel's maid, who quarrelled bitterly with her and wanted to ruin her reputation. In fact the 200 boxes of papers arrived safely in London and were stored at 67 Baker Street which Isabel shared with her sister Dilly. It was Dilly who later weeded the collection and sent only seven large boxes to the muniment room in Wardour Castle.

But there is no doubt that Isabel did burn the translation of *The Scented Garden*. She justified this in a letter to the *Morning Post* in June 1891 saying that people might read it 'for filth's sake' and it put Richard's immortal soul at risk. He had ended the book with a chapter on the techniques of homosexual love-making which he considered to be worth studying, 'because nothing can be contrary to Nature, which includes all things.' Nevertheless, Isabel was worried that the book might fall into the wrong hands; 'my husband's *Scented Garden* would have become a Christmas book for boys on the plea that the mind should be trained to everything.'

Richard's coffin arrived in Liverpool aboard the *Palmyra* on 12 February 1891 and his funeral was held in the church of St Mary Magdalene at Mortlake on 16 June. Isabel's family were there in force. She set about raising money for a mausoleum[17] and writing the story

The Burton mausoleum in St Mary's churchyard at Mortlake where Richard and Isabel lie 'side by side in death', photographed in 2010.

of his life, much of it completed at Wardour. He had expressed a wish about his burial: 'I should like us both to lie in a tent, side by side.' Isabel had a tomb made of Forest of Dean stone and white Carrara marble, in the shape of an Arab tent with eight oriental lamps inside and a mixture of Christian and Islamic symbols on the walls. There, in St Mary's churchyard at Mortlake, she herself was place beside him after her death from cancer on 22 March 1896.

In her passionate letter to her mother in October 1859 Isabel wrote: 'you and my father are immensely proud of your families . . . . . but from the present to the future, I believe that our proudest record will be our alliance with Richard Burton.' Perhaps there was some truth in what she wrote.

12

The Disastrous Dowager

THIS ought to be a chapter of blank pages. When a historian can find almost nothing about the life of a person and only one-sided opinions about that person, he ought to pack up and do something else. Such is the problem with the old Dowager, widow of the 12th Lord. But she was important in the story of Wardour and cannot be ignored.

We know that Anne Lucy, Dowager Lady Arundell (1842-1934) was a disaster in the history of the Wardour estate. Everyone says so. Her reputation is almost unreservedly bad. But the details are missing. The family papers contain almost nothing of her years at Wardour as wife, widow and chatelaine of the castle and estate. There are no letters from her, no diaries, no papers justifying her bizarre behaviour. We do not know her side of the story at all. There is only one clear photograph of her, showing a young woman at about the time of her marriage to John Arundell in 1862. Her years at Wardour stretched from 1862 to 1934, an almost unbelievably long period of 72 years, and her legacy was bleak.[1]

When John, the last Lord Arundell revised and completed the history of his family in 1939, he struggled to find appropriate words to describe the damage inflicted by Anne Lucy. There are three drafts of his paragraphs in the archives, each an attempt to tone down the anger and bitterness he felt. This is one version:[2]

The only known, clear picture of Anne Lucy Errington, wife of the 12th Lord,
presumably at the time of her marriage in 1862.

Unfortunately, she was a person singularly ill fitted to govern a landed estate. Narrow-minded, conceited and obstinate, she was also an easy prey to the parasites she encouraged and the mismanagement that she allowed or may even be said to have fostered. Her character was a mass of inconsistencies. A bigoted Catholic, she dismissed Catholic tenants and replaced them by Protestants. Acclaimed and acclaiming herself a clever woman of business, she sold landed property and old family furniture at ridiculously low prices to gratify her passion for huckstering[3] and her own private fortune was largely depleted in spite of the fact that her household was conducted on utterly inadequate lines.

Although she encumbered the estates with Land Improvement charges amounting to £1,300 per annum, the farmers were unable to get the most necessary repairs executed and the gardens were let to a man who neglected and impoverished them in every way. On the day after her funeral, Mr. John Arundell (the 15th Lord's son) and his solicitor Mr. Cecil Turner,[4] counted 23 places where the rain had penetrated through the roof of the mansion.

During her life, she sold a very large portion of the furniture in the castle and by her will she directed that all the pictures not heirlooms (of which she had inherited the whole from the Arundell family) and all the china in the house (a very considerable part of which belonged to the Arundell family) should be sold for the purposes of her will.[5]

It must, however, be recorded in her favour that she made Mr. John Arundell an allowance to enable him to go to Oxford and provided for its continuance till he should inherit the estates.

Although the 15th Lord and his family lived in the east wing of the mansion, having been established there by the 12th Lord, she maintained no relations with him and had not spoken to him during the last fifteen years of her life.[6] Land was sold at ridiculously low prices in the very centre of the property. Lady Arundell herself initiated the sales of the following farms and holdings: Leigh Court

Farm, the watercress beds next to Dengrove Copse, the Castle Inn and adjoining land at Brookwater, West-End Farm, the New Inn at Donhead, Conduit Farm, the Arundell Arms Inn and land at Ansty, a large pasture adjoining Mansfield Farm besides numerous cottage properties. All these sites were enclosed on all sides by the Wardour Estate.

Anne Lucy Errington came from a staunchly Catholic family living at High Warden near Hexham in Northumberland. She married John, the eldest son of the 11th Lord on 13 October 1862 but six days later his father died. Martina Hoskins,[7] a parlour maid at Wardour in the 1930s remembered being told: 'The old Dowager was Miss, Mrs. and Lady all in one week.' The newly-weds were called back from honeymoon for the funeral. The greatest sadness for the couple was that no children were born to them. Local people predicted that this would happen because, 'when the hatchments were erected at the castle on the death of the 11th Lord, one of them fell and an old superstition said that because of this no heir would be born.'

The household in 1861 consisted of 18 servants, ranging from Emma Higgs, age 49, the housekeeper, to Joseph Gurd age 18, the pageboy. There were two footmen, three housemaids, two laundry maids and two kitchen maids. Only one was born in Wardour as the convention was to employ servants from distant places so they would not gossip with their families about their employer's affairs. In 1881 there were only 9 servants, in 1891 14 and in 1901, 10. The estate consisted of 6,037 acres and produced an income of £8,949 in 1865 (£450,000 in 2010 values).[8] This had shrunk to £6,253 in 1904,[9] an indication perhaps that the 12th Lord was no more adept at estate management than his predecessors. Ordinary price inflation had been 25% during that time.

We do not know much about life at Wardour during these years. After the 12th Lord's death in 1906 his widow published a book of his speeches and introduced them with a brief account of his life. She said he was 'a thorough sportsman, a lover of nature, a staunch

Conservative, actively opposed to Home Rule,[10] unfortunately not gifted as an orator, a book lover . . . ' He strongly opposed the development of democracy and Sir William Harcourt's death duties legislation.[11] Many of his speeches, including some to his tenants in Tisbury, refer to the need for society to recognise 'the inequality which is inevitable among men', and the benefits of rule by aristocrats. His tenants must have been on the edge of their seats with excitement.

The 12th Lord was a good shot and keen huntsman who

The 12th Lord Arundell

followed hounds till a few years before his death. Jack Mullins' father was coachman to the old Dowager and remembered that she always rode side-saddle to the hunt. Every day Lord Arundell sat for an hour on a seat outside the north door of the castle so that any tenant or employee could tackle him on any subject. In 1885 he gave the Guildhall to Wardour, for dances, whist drives and bazaars. In 1896 Lady Arundell gave the land for a new church at Tisbury, opened in November 1898.[12] In 1900 they sold the four Reynolds portraits from the Music Room for £11,500 (£700,000 in 2010 values). Apparently they were a devoted couple. Lady Arundell wrote in 1909, 'I can truthfully say he was the best and most devoted of husbands, the most genial companion, the most considerate of neighbours, always courteous and hospitable.'

One local family who might have enjoyed hospitality at the castle were the Kiplings but probably they never met because the Arundells had nothing in common with them. Rudyard's parents, Lockwood and

Alice, came to live in Tisbury at The Gables in 1893, mainly because of their friendship with the artistic Wyndham family at Clouds House in East Knoyle. They loved visiting Old Wardour Castle and when Rudyard arrived from America with his family in 1894, to spend three months near his parents, he rented the house called Arundells in Tisbury and wrote to an American friend, 'The climate is only fit for marine monsters ... but I am promised all the fishing I like on Arundell's grounds. This consoles me a little.'[13] It would be interesting to know what the Arundells thought of the Kiplings. There is no record that they were ever received at the castle[14] although Lockwood frequently took visitors to the old castle and signed the Visitor's Book.[15] In 1900 Rudyard finished writing *Kim* and his father used people on the Wardour estate to pose as models for him to make the illustrations.

The 12th Lord died on 26 October 1906 in London where he had gone to vote against the Education Bill which he feared would reduce the influence of the Churches over education. Then the troubles began.

A group at Wardour School in the 1890s with one of the nuns of the Sisters of Charity who ran the school.

In the 1890s the 12th Lord developed a will-making mania. In the final version, signed on 8 February 1905, his will ran to 77 pages and included 12 codicils.[16] He was obviously worried about the future of the estate when it seemed likely that there would be no male heir to the title. His brother Everard was a 71 year old Jesuit priest, his cousin Edgar age 46 was married to a 45 year old widow and had no children; his other cousin Gerald was 44 and unmarried. After Gerald, there were in 1905 no more male heirs to the title. What he could not know, when he made the will, was that Gerald would marry in 1906 and have three children including a son who would eventually inherit the title.[17]

Therefore, the 12th Lord made a will leaving the whole estate, castle and contents to his widow for life, 'without impeachment of waste' i.e. hers to do with as she wished, except for listed family heirlooms which were to pass with the title. On her death the whole estate was to pass to any surviving holders of the title and their male heirs. But if the title become extinct the whole property should go to the eldest son of his goddaughter, Mabile Mary Talbot. She was the granddaughter of the 9th Lord who was orphaned at the age of 11 and married her distant cousin Reginald Talbot in 1898. They came to live on the Wardour estate and had a son Reginald in 1900, the first of their eleven children. It seems extraordinary that a will settlement made in 1905 could determine the descent of the estate far into the future but such an arrangement is legally possible unless an heir in the future bars the entail and converts the estate to an unencumbered estate in fee simple, for him to leave as he wishes. [18]

It is not difficult to imagine how trouble soon began when the old Dowager refused to move, on the death of her husband, from the main apartments of the castle to a smaller house on the estate. Gerald (who inherited the title as the 15th Lord in 1921) came to live in the east wing with his wife and three young children. Tensions developed because there were signs that the Dowager was selling family heirlooms listed in the 1907 inventory.[19] Isabel, the last Lord's sister, remembered many years later:[20] 'Life became unbearable for my parents . . . they had to watch pantechnicons of pictures and furniture being loaded for sale in London.' Gerald took her to the High Court in 1913 and she was ordered to cease such activity and restore the items. Another similar case reached the High Court in 1931 involving the sale of portraits, miniatures, the Gerald Douw picture, silver spoons and candlesticks, with the same result.[21]

However, the worst cause of trouble was Anne Lucy's determination to make Wardour Castle Chapel a private chapel and to exclude the public from services there.[22] This was odd as her husband had set up a Trust to look after the chapel for local use. Presumably she regarded the new church in Tisbury as adequate for the parish. The arguments began in 1924 with the old Dowager claiming that as owner of the whole castle building surrounding the chapel, she could decide the times of services and the seating of the congregation because access to the chapel was through her property. The case went to the High Court

The priest at Wardour, probably Father Dupay, leaving the presbytery, to visit parishioners on horseback, c. 1890.

again, the Dowager stopped payment to the priests and disappeared for over a year to a secret address. Father Wolfe, the parish priest wrote to Lord Arundell in 1924, 'if there is a Purgatory at all, some people will catch it <u>hot</u> later on . . . how tired I am of Wardour affairs.' The Bishop intervened, refused to allow the Dowager to take Holy Communion in the chapel and referred the case to Rome as it was beyond a local solution. Anne Lucy disappeared again. The decision from Rome was that the chapel should remain as a parish and not a private chapel so the Dowager set off for Rome to see the Pope and beg for his mercy. The result is not known.

The sadness of these years can be easily imagined. The estate was neglected. In 1935 the income from the estate was £6,066,[23] less than it had been in 1904 and nearly £3,000 less than in 1865. The 15th Lord wrote to his solicitor in February 1927:

> What a great deal of unnecessary trouble Lady Arundell has given us all in seeking to have her own way. I hear bad reports of her health, she is going downhill very fast, she never reads a paper and takes no interest in anything . . . she sleeps the greater part of the day . . . another thing she is constantly doing is to have a conversation with an imaginary dog when there is no dog in the room.[24]

In the event, Anne Lucy lived for another seven years. When she died on 24 October 1934 Les Parsons, the thatcher's son from Ansty, was at school in Wardour. He remembered how Father Hookway, the parish priest took all the children to stand around her deathbed and say prayers for the repose of her soul. John, the last Lord Arundell, wrote in his family history, 'It is a fact of melancholy significance that not one voice was raised to regret her passing on the estate which had been her home for 72 years.' There were no Arundell family mourners at her funeral in the castle chapel. But what is her side of the story? We shall never know.

13

Family Life at Wardour

By 1906 there had been very little laughter in Wardour Castle for over 50 years. The last family to live there with children was the 11th Lord's whose twelve children were at Wardour in the 1840s and 1850s. Thereafter, an increasingly lonely, childless couple, the 12th Lord and his wife, inhabited the whole castle. But in 1898 Gerald Arundell, who eventually became the 15th Lord, was invited by them to live in the east wing. He continued to do so after his marriage in 1906 and the birth of his children, John, Blanche and Isabel. Despite the problems of living next to the old Dowager, an increasingly eccentric recluse, family life was happy and energetic. There can be no better account of those years than the unpublished memories of their child Isabel, written in 1993 for her grandchildren:

> My parents could not have been more different. My father, very English, was slow and thorough, with a great sense of duty, and a love of the great outdoors. He was a first rate shot and cricketer, being a right-hand bat and a left-hand bowler. He liked fishing, and spent hours bird-watching. A great sportsman, he was expert at carpentry, but was rather serious and had a dread of getting into debt. My mother[1], on the other hand, was somewhat harum-scarum with a keen sense of the ridiculous, a hatred of hypocrisy, and an ability to make and keep friends. She was very extravagant, which was the only

Ivy Segrave, wife of the 15th Lord Arundell, as a young woman.

thing they rowed over. To this day the word 'anthracite' and 'laundry' give me cold chills. These bills would arrive at breakfast-time and lead to shouting matches, Daddy capping it by saying 'Well, we'll have to leave Wardour'. What a thought! I used to pray 'Please God no anfursite bills', not knowing what the word meant. My mother was madly untidy, but luckily there were tallboys in most of the rooms, into which she shoved everything when the front door bell rang. Later, of course, she couldn't find anything.

My parents would have been happy in the east wing had it not been for Anne Lucy's constant interference. She had long wanted an heir to inherit Wardour, and was very jealous when my brother John was born. Previously, my mother had miscarried of a son due, she was sure, to Anne Lucy's unkindness. She was very narrow minded, and told Mama she mixed too much with her Protestant neighbours. If a girl on the estate got 'into trouble' her house was never visited. This was too much for my mother, who made a point of visiting the unfortunates and finding them congenial posts in service.

My mother had such charm. People loved her and still talk of her. She was the least snobbish person I ever met – people to her were friends, and their background unimportant. She could dislike people too, mainly snobs and affected people and anyone caught in a lie, but she usually managed to avoid them. She loved children too, and was such fun that they always came to her. We had a Christmas party each year for the Wardour school children, and a summer one at Old Wardour with prizes for races. I had to row them on the lake as first prize.

My mother had a wonderful cook, dear Mary Trim, who came to her straight from Wardour school. Mama, who couldn't boil an egg, somehow trained Mary to become a Cordon Bleu cook, and she was the only person I know who could make a delicious French omelette from powdered egg in World War II. Mary married John Harrison and went to live in Tisbury. Next, we had a temporary cook, a widow called Mrs. O'Boyle, who used to get the odd-job boy Harry Gurd to run errands for her. His family became worried about this, and his mother said 'Oi reken that ther Mrs. O'Boyle be arter our 'arry'. To my mother's great surprise they announced their engagement, and Mrs. O'Boyle, visiting Harry's mother, addressed her as 'mum'. 'Don't you go mummin' me' was the reply 'Thee's old enough to be his mum yourself.' They took an old cottage on the road to Donhead and opened a tiny shop there. It was a godsend to the Wardour people, as until then the nearest shops were in Tisbury.

To return to my father, he would walk me for miles and leave me exhausted and fractious.

Mrs Harris, the cook at Wardour in the 1930s.

Walking in the warren one day my father said 'If you put your ear to the ground, you will be able to hear the ram.' This was a pump which supplied water from the lakes to the castle. As we approached Pond Close he pointed to a little house, and said 'The ram is in there.' I could hear it snorting and hissing, and thinking of centaurs and other mythical beasts, I fled home in terror. Despite all these fears, walks with Daddy were always interesting. He gave me an abiding love of the countryside, particularly birds. We had a great variety in those days, before pesticides, herbicides, and the destruction of hedges.

I forgot to mention that, on my uncle's death, we acquired his groom, Welsh, and a cob and trap. I longed to ride so Mr Holloway, one of our tenants, lent me Kitty, a rather fat, grey pony. Being used on his farm, she would arrive muddy and unkempt but I learned to curry-comb her, brush her long tail (always matted) and polish her hooves until she looked a really high-class pony. Welsh started by taking me out for a couple of hours on the leading rein and, finding I could stay on, he released me and gave Kitty a resounding whack, thereupon she bolted and threw me. I soon mounted again and learned to hang on, having a good seat in the saddle. Unfortunately Kitty had a hard mouth, resulting in my being heavy-handed.

Oh, the fun we had then, we three, riding through the woods and on to the Downs – Kitty, Queenie (my black and white fox terrier) and me. Soon I learned to put Kitty over small jumps, a stream or a fallen log. Welsh, in the meantime, had blotted his copybook, by being permanently drunk. He lived up to his name, disappearing one day owing money everywhere. I was not sorry as I never liked him.

Charles Lever, an ex-cavalryman who rented one of our farms in Ansty, had mounted and taught John to ride, and even taught him tent-pegging,[2] so we often went out together. The gallops on the Downs from Crockerton Firs were most exhilarating – how Queenie kept up on her little legs, I do not know. I went on my first cub-hunt when I was about nine. Unfortunately, while drawing covert in Fonthill Woods, John's horse kicked out. Kitty dodged, and I got the full benefit on my left knee. I shall never forget the pain, lying in the bushes trying not to cry. John had to take me home, and my knee swelled and swelled, being measured each day. Daddy had to carry me into church, to my shame, for Christmas Mass. Luckily no permanent damage was done and I was soon hunting again, and Kitty became 'hooked'. If we were out hacking and she heard the hunting horn, I could not stop her joining the hunt, regardless of my not being dressed for the part, i.e. stock, boots and hard hat. She was very sure-footed, and easy to catch if I fell off. Her worst faults were galloping under low branches and charging through narrow gates, when I had to either crouch low on her withers or pull my legs up over the saddle.

John always staged plays for our mother's birthday. The one I remember best was with him as a millionaire, Blanche as, first, his housekeeper and, later a detective, and me as a burglar. I had to climb through a stage window and steal a lot of pennies. John thought his play was a serious masterpiece, and was deeply hurt when the audience started laughing when he said 'We will now go to bed', and he and his housekeeper shared one. My mother also staged tableaux, which I hated because I had to keep still. I had to recite 'The Little Vulgar Boy' from *The Ingoldsby Legends*, John lending me trousers for the occasion. They came down, and the audience thought it was part of the act.

We used to disguise ourselves to take in people. John started it by dressing in old ragged clothes, and opening the gate for people passing through to visit the Old Castle ruins. He bowed and Blanche and I curtsied and held out our hands for pennies. They used to dirty my face and pinch me to make me look deprived. John made quite a lot of money, Blanche got half, and I was left with bruises. Eventually our parents found out, and were horrified. John did very well on the

Stock Exchange in later life. Another time we visited the Presbytery at night, and John told a pitiful story of a father out of work, a dying mother, and great hunger. We were given ten shillings and a guilty conscience, so next day we took it back and explained ourselves. The priests thought it very funny and were amazed at our disguises.

My mother employed a boy to clean the boots and knives. The latter were steel, not stainless in those days and they were put in a machine with some pink powder and a handle was turned, a boring and tedious process. The boys came from Wardour School after lessons and before returning home. Mama decided to employ Bede Ridley and, with John and Blanche away at school, he became my younger brother. We climbed trees together and made tree houses, bird-nested and explored the woods. When I went to boarding school, he looked after all my animals. We had made all the hutches together. I had Queenie and a variety of her puppies, rabbits, guinea pigs, a jackdaw I had tamed, white mice and a rat. I hated leaving them but I knew Bede would tend to them. He used to write to me, telling me how they were doing and signing himself 'Your faithful carpenter'. Later, my mother found him a place as under footman with Lord Nelson at Trafalgar House.

When John was in his early teens he saved up some money, and got Anthony Foyle, a carpenter, to make him a boat. We kept it on Old Wardour lake, and what fun we had in it. One day John and Blanche got out, and kicked the boat with me in it out on the lake. I could not swim then and screamed with fright, John shouting instructions on how to row. At first I only rowed further out, but at last brought it ashore. A rather scary way of learning to row. I must have had a good guardian angel.

The Old Wardour lake froze most winters, and John taught me to skate. We took a gramophone on the ice, and eventually I was able to waltz with him. He was a really good skater, but I did a lot of falling about. What a wonderful childhood we had, walking the woods, hunting, shooting and skating, noticing the change in the seasons, where rare flowers grew, and watching the habits of birds. There was an abundance of wildlife then, so collecting birds' eggs, taking only one, was permissible. I still recall the thrill of finding a long-tailed tit's nest, with its intricate work of lichen and cobwebs lined with down. Golden were those days at Wardour long ago – beautiful the land and friendly the people.

Martina Hoskins, parlourmaid in the 1930s confirmed this description of happy family life. The castle had not been modernised. There were oil lamps and candles in all the rooms and only one bathroom. Hot water was carried to the bedrooms by housemaids. Martina's duties involved waiting at table and that meant a change of uniform each day, from blue dress with white cap and apron in the mornings to green dress with coffee coloured cap and apron in the afternoons.[3] The family entertained a lot, especially at weekends and Martina remembered that Lady Arundell usually wore a white satin evening dress and tiara for dinner when there were guests. There were always silver candlesticks on the table and six or seven courses.

Martina felt great affection for Lord and Lady Arundell and the children; 'they treated us all as part of their family, we shared their joys and we shared their sorrows. Lady Arundell was like a mother to me.'[4] Whenever there were young guests, the children organised the Bath Races which meant careering down the stone stairs between attics and first floor in a hip bath. The great skill was to pull on the banisters at the right time so that the bath and passenger landed in the gallery. Lord Arundell eventually banned the sport because of damage to the walls. Equally exciting perhaps, were the regular dances organised by Isabel on the castle roof in the moonlight. The roof was also used by the young people for sunbathing in the buff in those memorable hot summers of the 1920s and 1930s.

Back to Isabel's memories:

Our nearest neighbours were the Douglas-Hamiltons at Ferne, six miles away. The Duke was crippled and very difficult to understand, but the Duchess[5] I adored. She had brought up her seven children to sunbathe and to wear no shoes or socks, and I persuaded Mummy to let me do likewise. I first went over there when I was aged about three and I was intensely shy. Mairi, six months younger, stuck her tongue out at me, which didn't help. I found her big brothers somewhat overpowering.

Ferne was always full of the bustle of dogs and children, and in time, having overcome my shyness, I came to love it and Mairi became my dearest friend. She radiated life and was expert at everything she did. She played *The Moonlight Sonata* exquisitely, was a good artist, rode both astride and side-saddle, swam, skied, and was most athletic. They say the seventh child of a seventh child develops second sight, and this was certainly true in her case. She used to tell me she would never live to be grown up, and three months before her thirteenth birthday she told her sister Margaret not to bother about a present, as she would not live to be thirteen. I was at school when my mother visited me to tell me the news. Mairi had been jumping her dogs over some garden benches, fell, banged her nose, and erysipelas had set in, followed by pneumonia, and she was dead within a fortnight. By her wish she was buried in the shrubbery among her favourite dogs.

In 1931 I was presented at Court. Wearing long white dresses with trains, and the Prince of Wales' emblem, the three feathers on their heads, the debutantes with their mothers moved slowly in cars up The Mall – to the ribald comments of the onlookers. In the throne room we were lined up to curtsy to the ground, first to King George V, and then to Queen Mary. The Princes stood behind the thrones, the Prince of Wales looking very bored. Among the VIPs beside the thrones, I picked out one and whispered 'Mummy, who is the fascinating man with white hair brushed over his ears?' I simply could not take my eyes off him. 'Shush, darling, that is Lloyd George[6], and don't ever tell your father you admire him.' I well understood how he fascinated the masses, and could not wait to get Daddy to grow his hair longer so I could brush it over his ears. He was so flattered by my attentions that he duly complied. When I had finished he said, 'By God, you have made me look like that damned Lloyd George.' I assured him he looked exactly like himself.

In everyone's opinion, John was the perfect heir for Wardour. He was devoted to the estate and grew up to love its people and its history. In addition, he had the intelligence and the sensitivity to make a success of managing such a large enterprise in the mid 20th century and was trained to do so. People believed he spoke the truth when he said at his 21st birthday garden party at Wardour in 1928:

> This is the place I most want to be and you are the people I most want to be with. As a little boy away at school and as a man at University, my thoughts have always strayed back to Wardour and wandered around its lanes picking out your faces. So it will always be in the days to come.[7]

John was educated at Stonyhurst in Lancashire, the direct descendant of the college at St. Omers where so many of his ancestors had been before him. He entered the school in May 1916 and was lucky to begin at Hodder, the Prep school, situated in a magnificent setting high above the River Hodder and overlooking unspoiled countryside. In the main school, to which he eventually transferred, there were about 300 boys and 20 Jesuit masters. The corridors were gas-lit, the dormitories vast and without hot or cold water. The curriculum was very old-fashioned with Science only for the few and very little music or art but one of John's contemporaries described it as 'an astonishingly liberal education.'[8] Boys were woken in early morning by a wooden

The 15th Lord and Lady Arundell with John and Isabel at the east door of New Wardour Castle in 1929.

rattle and then there was silence between waking up and Grace in the Refectory before breakfast. There was daily Mass for the whole school. Few parents made visits and many boys did not see their parents for years because they were serving in India and other parts of the Empire.

Corporal punishment was very frequent and the standard of teaching was mediocre until the arrival of Father Bellanti in 1922. As Prefect of Studies he made great improvements. John was not a high flier but he won prizes, was very prominent in the Debating Society and was regarded by contemporaries as an intellectual. Tom Burns, one of John's friends recalled that there was no bullying at the school and the Jesuits were nearly all kind.[9] The chapel played a central part in all their lives.

John left Stonyhurst in July 1926 and entered the very different world of New College, Oxford where he studied Modern History. Once again he was in surroundings of great beauty. A fellow undergraduate recalled that the college was 'the almost exclusive preserve of the English ruling class' and 'more like living in some large and pleasant country house than attending an educational institution.'[10] The austere but benevolent ex cabinet-minister, H.A.L. Fisher presided over the college and there was a lively awareness of socialism, thanks to the presence of Dick Crossman and Douglas Jay as tutors.[11] It may be that some of John's keen social awareness developed in these days. John's career at Oxford was uneventful, academically and socially. He became keen on rowing and rowed in the Second College Eight in 1927, '28, and '29, an activity he continued in the 1930s as a member of the Thames Rowing Club.

When he left Oxford John took a year's agricultural course at Cambridge and thus became the best ever qualified Arundell in terms of farming and forestry. He then went to work on the London Stock Exchange but as soon as his father inherited the estate, on the death of the old Dowager in 1934, he returned to Wardour and helped to repair some of the damage caused by long years of neglect. Lord Arundell handed over the estate to his son to avoid another round of death duties and together they threw themselves into estate improvements. John took particular pleasure in sorting the archives and making a catalogue of them. When he took his seat in the House of Lords on 13 June 1939, a few months after the death of his father, all seemed set fair for the future of Wardour. But the storm clouds were gathering in Europe.

14

Wardour in Wartime

ON 1 September 1939 Germany invaded Poland. Two days later Britain and France declared war on Germany and the world was changed for ever.

John Arundell had always wanted to be a full-time soldier and he applied for a commission in September 1929 but the old Dowager vetoed his application and threatened to cut off his allowance so he went to study agriculture at Cambridge. A few years later John applied for a commission in the Territorial Army, was accepted and joined the 4th Battalion of the Wiltshire regiment. The application records that he was 71 inches high, weighed 162 lb, spoke French and German and had travelled throughout Europe and Canada[1]

Territorial duties were fairly light and entailed an evening's training in some weeks and a two week summer camp. By the time war broke out, John had been promoted to captain and was attached to the 2nd Battalion. In August 1939 they were on manoeuvres at Catterick Camp in Yorkshire and the battalion was ordered to mobilise and be ready for embarkation within two weeks, as part of the British Expeditionary Force. Martina Hoskins, the castle parlourmaid, remembered that she polished John's uniform buttons before saying goodbye.[2]

The battalion of about 800 men landed at Cherbourg on 14 September. Eight months of waiting and watching lay ahead. John led a company of about 200 men and they were stationed near Lille where they dug defences as part of the Gort Line, intended to repel a sudden German invasion. So quiet was the situation that in January 1940 men began to go on leave to England. John's turn came in March when he spent five days at home and said goodbye for the last time.

In early May the battalion made plans to pack up and move to Norway but before much could be done, Hitler ordered the German invasion of the Low Countries on 10 May. The Belgians planned to defend a line from Antwerp to Namur; the French thought they were safe behind the Maginot Line so the thirteen British divisions (about 150,000 ill-equipped men) were expected to hold the gap and prevent a German advance to the sea, if they made a breakthrough.

The 2nd battalion was stationed between Hal and the river Dyle but not for long. The German advance was astonishingly fast and by 16 May they had swept through all opposition and were only 40 miles east of Amiens. John, as a company commander, led his 200 men in retreat. The roads were blocked with soldiers, vehicles and guns; the men carried all their equipment and were starving. Meanwhile, the Germans reached the sea and the great fear at the British Headquarters was that they would then sweep north east and cut off the British forces. There would then be no escape to the sea.

John and his men were ordered to dig in along the river Scarpe near Roeux. On 22 May they were shelled and bombed all day and night. The battalion commander, on his own initiative, ordered a retreat from Roeux to Gavrelle. John was captured on the morning of 23 May as he and his men made their way between the two towns. He had a small wound on his left arm but it soon healed. On 28 May the Belgians surrendered, the remnants of the 2nd battalion reached Lille and made their way to Dunkirk where only 270 out of the 800 men were rescued from the beaches on 31 May.

For the next four years, John was moved from one prison camp to another.[3] He escaped successfully from Eichstatt in June 1943 but

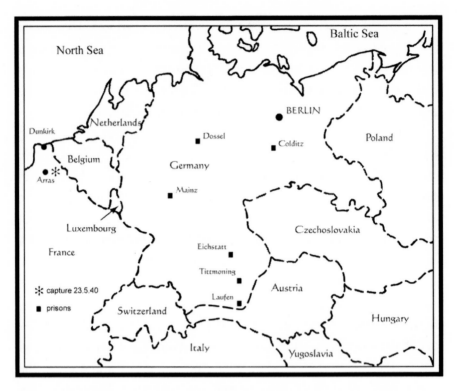

Map to show where John Arundell was captured near Arras in 1940 and his places of imprisonment in Germany.

was recaptured and spent almost a year in Colditz. His prisoner of war number was 383.

It is very difficult now to imagine the conditions in the camps which varied greatly, from Dulag XII (Mainz), a Transit Camp, to Oflag IVc (Colditz) which has achieved almost mythical status. Apart from the deprivation of food and basic comfort, one major problem was boredom; how to get through the days and weeks and months without going mad. A.N.L. Munby[4] was with John in Oflag VIIc (Laufen) and recalled that John kept himself occupied by making notes on Italian painting and the Beveridge Plan;[5] he wrote elaborate menus in French for dinners where the greatest delicacy was sardines from a Red Cross food parcel and he looked after the prisoners' Library. One of the prisoners wrote these lines:

When Arundell discusses the Pictorial
His manner is urbane, though grand seigneurial;
But acting as Librarian
Makes him quite totalitarian
The old Noblesse becomes New Dictatorial.[6]

Meanwhile at Wardour, the castle was more full of people than at any time since it sheltered the French refugee clergy in the 1790s. From 1939 to 1945 the east wing housed nearly 50 evacuee children who were looked after by the Sisters of Nazareth. Their mission, at their house in Southampton, was to care for children in need; some were orphans, others came from broken or very disturbed homes. On 31 July 1939 two sisters visited Wardour Castle to view the accommodation offered them by Lord Arundell, in case evacuation was ordered from Southampton, which was likely to be bombed. The private diary[7] of the sisters records their visit:

> The Sisters were kindly received by Lady Arundell who expressed her pleasure at having Catholic evacuees, especially little boys. The accommodation seemed rather limited for all our children and the sanitary arrangements left much to be desired. Besides, there is no electric light or gas, only paraffin lamps, and no means of heating the big rooms in winter except by small fires. The one great advantage is that the children would have every opportunity of practising their religion; there is a beautiful chapel and the school is conducted by the Sisters of Charity.

I contacted three of the evacuees[8] recently and one of them, Brian Osborne, remembers those days with mixed feelings. The evacuation to Wardour took place on 2 September 1939. The 84 boys and six sisters were transported with all their luggage, including mattresses and bedclothes, in two buses and a lorry. At the end of the month the 40 'babies' (those under 6 years old) were transferred to Swansea, because of overcrowding, but some of the older ones returned later.

I remember my bed was by a blocked up, large fireplace and at night when the wind blew, the noise sounded like a banshee howling. It was very frightening. There were about ten boys in each room. All things had to be shared so no one had a box or cupboard for themselves. There were no books or toys. At night we used chamber pots but in the day time there was a large shed with several seats inside;[9] a large hole was dug and every now and then, when it got full, a fresh one was dug by the boys. There was a room for washing, I think it had been used as the scullery; it had sinks down one side and a long shallow trough down the other. We had all-over washes in cold water each day.

Brian Osborne as an altar server at Wardour chapel, taken when he was an evacuee at the castle in 1942.

The sister in charge was Sister Ann. She was very strict and had a cane and was not shy in using it on hands and bottoms. Boys who swore, saying 'Bloody' had their mouths washed out with soap and sometimes they were made to stand in a corner. One sister I remember especially was Sister Boniface. She was gentle, kind and when the other sisters were not looking she'd give you a cuddle. School was at Wardour. We were taught by the Sisters of Charity. We attended chapel twice a day and on Sunday three times. Father Hyland

and Father Flynn were the parish priests, they took great interest in helping the children.

When we were not at school and had spare time we had to help clean the place, darn our socks and clean shoes (we only wore them in winter). We would have to go to bed in winter at seven o'clock and summer at eight or nine. We played in a large field at the back of the house, the only outside area we were allowed to play in. I remember walking to it in summer in bare feet. We had to walk along a path that had beech trees on each side and where the beech nuts fell it was hard on the feet. There were a lot of wooden hoops and we played with them and we made ships out of string and sticks. We were taken for walks to Old Wardour Castle but as far as I can remember, never to Tisbury.

At Christmas we did get a little present, an orange or an apple with a few nuts. We had to go up the Music Room at the top of the stairs to get them. One Christmas we put on a little play for some soldiers who were camped at the front. The play was St. George and the Dragon and it took place in the Saloon. I took the part of St George. We never saw much of Lady Arundell who was living in the main part of the house.

Unfortunately, all John's letters home to his family during the years of imprisonment have been lost[10] so we have to use other accounts for a record of those grim days and for the famous escape from Eichstatt.[11] John was in the Eichstatt camp for nine months and the escape took place on the night of 3/4 June 1943. Sixty five men successfully breathed the fresh air of freedom in the early morning of 4 June. The tunnel began on the tiled floor of a staircase toilet and came out in a small chicken hut beside the prison fence on the road to Munich. The engineer of this brilliant construction was Lt. Jock Hamilton-Baillie, known by the guards as 'theatre-girl' from his role as leading lady in Coward's *Blithe Spirit*. The tunnel took many months to build and was equipped with lights

A sketch by Lieut. I. MacAskie of the entrance to the escape tunnel at Eichstatt where John and 64 others escaped on the night of 3 June 1943.

and an air supply. The 40 tons of spoil were carried out at night in sacks suspended from the prisoners' necks by straps under their great coats. John was escapee No. 37 and he and No. 36, the Hon. David Fellowes, set out through the woods together, sleeping by day and travelling at night and hoping to reach the Swiss border, 100 miles to the south west.

When the escape was discovered, the Germans launched a massive Home Guard search operation. Unfortunately all the escapees were captured within a few days. Many reported that villagers had treated them kindly and offered them free drinks before informing the police. All the prisoners were then punished for fourteen days in the old castle of Willibaldsburg on the outskirts of Eichstatt. They were kept in white-washed dungeons under 24 hour guard and then transferred to Colditz, the special prison for persistent troublemakers.

It is now very difficult to separate myth from reality in the story of Colditz, so greatly does it resonate in British memory. It is almost possible to forget it was a prison and to regard it as a sort of public school training camp with very strict rules and high spirited occupants. A few facts and figures: there were 50,000 Allied prisoners in camps all over Germany and Colditz had only 205 British and about 33 Free French prisoners while John was there. The castle had over 700 rooms but only those around an inner courtyard were used; it had been built as a hunting lodge for the Kings of Saxony and then became a mental hospital. It was chosen as a special camp because it was believed to be 'escape-proof' since it was in central Germany about 90 miles south of Berlin and surrounded by dense forests (despite this, 316 escape attempts were made). It was the German 'show' camp, the only one where prisoners were treated strictly according to the Geneva Convention and where the only punishment was solitary confinement.

The prisoners' courtyard at Colditz castle where John spent 10 months in 1943-44. (Imperial War Museum, HU20288)

Appels (roll calls) preceded by loud sirens were held frequently in the central courtyard, guards with Alsatian dogs patrolled the perimeter, the castle was flood-lit at night and there were bars at all the windows. There was no compulsory work because this was a prison for officers and therefore boredom was a major problem. One of the inmates later wrote that the castle could easily have become a prison full of mentally unbalanced men; the signs were all too obvious

The 7 a.m. roll call at Colditz sketched by Lieut. John Watton and showing John in shorts on the left, despite the freezing weather.

– first, a prisoner would become obsessed with a topic of study in the Library, then there was a fanatical pursuit of physical fitness, then a neglect of washing and finally, a mental breakdown.

Perhaps, worst of all, was the diet which led to extreme weakness and depression – for breakfast: coffee substitute (made from acorns) and bread; for lunch, potatoes and turnips (total 900 gms.) with 250 gms. of meat on Sundays; for supper, bread (300 gms.) and jam substitute. If it had not been for the Red Cross parcels which arrived regularly it is difficult to see how the men would have survived long.

The International Red Cross in Geneva was encouraged to make regular visits to the camp because Hitler was keen to prove that Germany was treating prisoners according to the rules. On 8 November 1943, when John was there, two Swiss doctors visited Colditz and sent a report to headquarters.[12] The rooms were each occupied by ten to fourteen officers, and the heating was not adequate. There were three special prisoners known as Prominente (the Earl of Hopetoun, Capt. Alexander and Giles Romilly, Churchill's nephew[13]). They were kept in separate rooms, locked and monitored three or four times each night. In the whole prison the electric light was very weak and the water supply did not reach the upper floors. The food was the same as at the other camps with fresh vegetables only rarely. The men were really fed by the contents of Red Cross parcels. Each officer had two uniforms supplied by the Red Cross. There were only a few things to buy in the shop but no toothpaste or writing equipment. Each prisoner was given a bottle of beer per week. A man could have a hot shower once every fortnight.

The doctors reported that the Infirmary at this time contained eight sick people, none serious. The two British doctors were not allowed to practise, for security reasons. The Library was reasonably equipped, there was a small orchestra and plays were produced but since there were no costumes, the prisoners made them from crepe paper and asked for more. The sports ground could be used for two hours per day and prisoners could go for two, hour-long walks each day. A British priest conducted services regularly. Discipline was very severe because all the inmates had tried to escape from other camps but the Commandant was thought to be fair. At the end, the doctors listed 28 individual complaints

Kriegsgefangenenlager **OFLAG IVc English Content** Datum **27.6.43**
Prisoner of War Camp — Date

Name **LORD ARUNDELL of WARDOUR** Vorname **JOHN FRANCIS**
Surname — Christian Name

Dienstgrad u. Truppenteil **CAPTAIN**
Rank and Unit

Geburtsdatum **18 JUNE 1907** Geburtsort **WILTSHIRE**
Date of birth — Native-place

Letzter Wohnort **OFLAG VII B**
Last dwelling

Adresse meiner Angehörigen **WARDOUR CASTLE**
Home Address

TISBURY   WILTS

Unverwundet — leicht verwundet — in deutsche Kriegsgefangenschaft geraten —
Unwounded — slightly wounded — prisoner of war in Germany —

befinde mich wohl.
I am well.

(Nichtzutreffendes ist zu streichen) **ARUNDELL of WARDOUR**
(Passages non apposite to the point to be cancelled) Signature

A postcard, partially completed by John in Colditz and intended for his mother but never sent and now in the Red Cross Archives in Geneva.

from the prisoners and all were answered with explanations of why nothing could be done or promises to investigate further.

In the absence of his letters, there is very little direct information about John's time in Colditz. We know he had a reputation for excessive exercise.[14] He became a fitness fanatic, although the meagre diet was not appropriate for such a regime. He was an enthusiastic member of the Drama group and helped with many of the plays. We know he received letters from the agent at Wardour, Major Floyd, because they are now in the family archives, stamped with the Colditz post room seal.[15] Presumably they were returned to Wardour with John's possessions when he was repatriated. In one letter from 1943, Major Floyd told John about the need for a new reservoir at Wardour and the problem of blocked drains caused by the evacuees in the east wing. Estate income was healthy and savings in 1943 were £7,559.16.9d. In another letter on 5 December 1943 Major Floyd explained the problem of the new tenant at Lower Farm in Ansty. He wanted to re-possess the field along

Squalls Lane, known as Sangers, which belonged to the farm but which the Misses Parsons of Spilsbury Farm had rented for some time. The new tenant said that Lower Farm was too small without the field. The Parsons had neglected the field for many years and it had reverted to scrub. But the Parsons opposed any change and had been to Wardour to see Lady Arundell. Lord Arundell was asked for his decision. We can only hope that this link with affairs at Wardour gave John some comfort in the bleak days in prison.

Ellison Platt was chaplain in Colditz and kept a diary. He recorded on Tuesday 1 February 1944:[16]

'Wardour for Washing!' So ran the legend on the eight foot banner which was paraded round the *Hof* this afternoon preceded by a band. It was John Arundell of Wardour's retirement from the post of laundry officer, and other placards were carried by sandwichmen. 'Peer's Soap' was a caricature of Lord Arundell bent over a wash tub. Another announced 'Arundell Laundry 1066-1944'. A third, another excellent caricature, showed my Lord driving a two-horse fly with great aplomb – his moustache and nose as true to life as life itself – with the caption, 'Arundell Delivers Today'. After the procession, John was chaired and borne round the courtyard. Bill Burton, the present laundry officer, pretended great indignation, but knew all too well that all the king's horses could not drag John Arundell to the position again.

We do not know when John became ill with TB but on 18 April 1944 he was moved to Obermassfeld Military Hospital and then to Elsterhorst. Sir Martin Gilliat[17] who suffered nightmares about Colditz until his death in 1993 remembered John in those days in the camp:

I remember him for his kindness – his splendid sense of humour, his courage in adversity and the uncomplaining way he battled on from day to day with health and strength gradually failing. John must have felt appallingly ill in those last months but he never complained and was really extremely apologetic and ashamed when quite rightly he was repatriated. Characteristically he promised that on his return home he would see the next of kin of all of us and give them a full report.[18]

Another friend, John Hamilton-Baillie, the engineer of the Eichstatt tunnel and fellow prisoner in Colditz, wrote in 1982:

I remember him as a kind, quiet, rather retiring man who drove himself hard to keep fit. I think of him being up early in the morning, taking a cold shower and jogging around the courtyard before there were many other people there. He was a gallant and much loved man.

At some stage the Red Cross Medical Commission recommended that John should be repatriated and on 5 September 1944 he was put on board a Military Hospital Train, Lzrt. Zug No 1114 v. 2123, bound for Gothenburg in Sweden. He eventually reached Liverpool but died at Chester on 25 September[19] as described in the Prologue. His family was around his bedside.

A cartoon sketch of John drawn by a fellow prisoner in Colditz and preserved by Col. P Storie – Pugh who was also imprisoned there.

Lady Arundell received many letters of condolence and this one from a fellow prisoner, the earl of Hopetoun, is in the family archives:

Dear Lady Arundell,

It was a great shock to us here to learn that John had died in England. To you it will be easy to understand how much we loved him, and for us it is heartbreaking to know how much you will miss him, and how much you will have longed to have him with you again. With others who are with me here, I had been with him since the dark days of 1940, and with them John will live on whenever we need the example of his high courage and chivalry. Always one thinks of him and will think of him when there is warm friendship, rich appreciation of life, sympathy and wit. He gave us all these things to a degree unsurpassed by anyone else I have ever met. It is true to say that John had no enemies; he was better known as a character than anyone else and all who met him loved him. In the life of these prison camps one literally leans on such characters, for without them life would have no highlights. John was a highlight. He gave us laughter, courtesy and sympathy, and helped not by what he did, for there is little to do, but by being always his great self. He managed by his courage and high character to preserve for himself and therefore for us all a link with universal values, which are so easily forgotten in surroundings like these. This is the service which John has rendered for those who were fortunate enough to be his friends and acquaintances during the last four years. Life is so much the poorer without him. Only those who knew him and know what he did for us all, can appreciate it. He has left behind accumulated reserves of his great heart in the memories of his friends, which will be carried by us for the rest of our lives. To you who have suffered such a great loss and to all of you who loved him at home, I send my deepest sympathy.

John made his will in August 1937[20] and set up a Trust Fund of £6,000 (£200,000 in 2010 values) for the relief of poverty, sickness, distress and unemployment among the tenants and residents of the Wardour estate and the people of Tisbury. He explained his reasons:

My desire in this is to follow, if only in a modest way according to my means, the generous bequest of my illustrious ancestor Sir Matthew Arundell, to whom the idea of property was consistent only with the welfare of the poorest tenant on his estates.

Then, in November 1939 when he was serving in France he made a codicil to the will and listed the names of 22 people on the Wardour estate who were to receive specific legacies. It is perhaps most appropriate that these names should now appear at the end of this chapter in memory of John's kindness and his love of the Wardour estate and its people: Francis Fisher, Charles Lever, William Lever, Samuel Clarke, Frederick Sanger, Silas Asprey, Herbert Lever, Reginald Jay, Leo Harrison, Charles Foyle, Joseph Randall, George Gurd, Frederick Gurd, Jack Mullins, Joseph Lever, Mark Harrison, Isabel Austridge, Richard Randall, Herbert Woods, Maud Mullins, Martina Mullins, Martina's father. May they rest in peace.

Reflections

I F Henry VIII were to return to earth for a short visit and decide to hold a tournament on Cranborne Chase and command the attendance of the descendants of the courtiers who settled in south west Wiltshire and north Dorset in the 16th century and who still live there today, he would be amazed at the response. Not only would there be present the Arundells of Wardour but also the Herberts of Wilton, the Thynnes of Longleat, the Seymours of Maiden Bradley, the Cecils of Cranborne ('I knew my chief clerk of the Court of Common Pleas would do well,' might be the King's comment), the Ashleys of Wimborne St. Giles and the Strangways of Melbury. There they all are, the descendants of Henry's courtiers who all acquired extensive estates in the great upheavals of the 16th century.

The King might ask how it could be that since his great landownership revolution in the 1530s, there had been only a slow and gradual change in landownership. How could England be so deeply conservative and traditional for 500 years? He would, of course, need to have it explained that taxation and death duties imposed on landowners for the sake of social and economic justice had made inroads on their wealth and reduced their ancestral acres. But most are still extremely wealthy and the gap between rich and poor is still very wide. Henry would need to be told that he was an aberration and that England is normally very slow to change. If this study has done nothing else it has confirmed the truth of Disraeli's remark: 'It is difficult, if not impossible, to ruin a family well rooted in the land.'

There have been two major barriers to my empathy with the Arundells —I have had a struggle to understand why it was necessary to build the largest Georgian mansion in Wiltshire; and an even greater struggle to understand how they could have allowed such vast debts to accumulate.

I know that it was considered necessary for a landowner to display magnificence appropriate to rank. It was an obligation. You couldn't let the side down. You had to build and decorate and furnish a house according to your station in life. But the Arundells had the chance to be different. For over 120 years they had managed with a modest house at Wardour, a small manor house in Hampshire and a house in London and against that background, the 3rd Lord achieved the greatest political power of any Arundell, ever. Throughout this period, the Penal Laws made it impossible for the Arundells to exercise the local or national power that aristocrats assumed was naturally theirs. Why then build a great mansion that was supposed to be the advertisement for such power? If only the Arundells could have diverged from convention and used their vast wealth for greater good.

Perhaps the impulse for a rich family to build a mansion lies deep in the human psyche. Even in our more egalitarian times, two enormous mansions have been completed recently by multi-millionaires, within a few miles of Wardour. I find that puzzling when a family needs only a modest house to live a good and happy life.

I have also struggled to understand the 8th and 10th Lords' attitude to debt, although the national events occurring when I wrote this have made it somewhat easier, with bankers and hedge-fund managers operating outside normal morality. 'There's a scarcity of money about' was a phrase the Arundells and their advisers often used. Did they never relate the shortage of money to their own credit-worthiness, which plummeted as their interest payments could not be met and loans were never repaid? There is something grossly immoral about debt if it is never associated by the debtors with the real people whose lives they have ruined; people like old Knight, the agent in Somerset and tradesmen in Tisbury and Salisbury. Henry may have felt deep guilt for the suffering he caused but he did not record it on paper and the sales of land were forced on him by the law. An old man wrote to Henry in August 1802, asking for the money he was owed, 'where all growing old you no my lord and I think you ought to be Made Ashamed in some public Court of Justice.... I wish that time was to come again where I wd. Make you more ashamed than ever you was . . .' There is no record of Henry's reply.

Aristocracy – the word is almost archaic now. What an extraordinary concept it is: that certain families by reason of blood and titles and wealth should have the right to rule the rest of us. The 12th Lord began writing a book on the subject, so keen was he to support the concept. He made speeches in Tisbury and elsewhere to explain that 'all men are unequal in height, strength, vigour, capacity . . . inequality and not equality is intended to be the law of the world . . . democracies will lapse into anarchy. In a democracy the dregs will come uppermost.' He was prepared to concede that all men have an equal right to justice and equality before the law and a right to respect 'according to their worth.' But titles were simply a recognition of inevitable inequality. How strange all of this reads in the 21st century but for most of our history aristocrats were accepted as the natural holders of power and authority. We are now out of line with a very long tradition.

It is probably as wrong to have favourites in the history of a family as for a teacher to have favourites in a class of pupils but if I were forced to choose, I would like to spend more time with Thomas the Valiant – what a knife-edge existence he led, combining loyalty to the monarchy and loyalty to his Church but he succeeded magnificently. I would like to have an hour's worth of discussion with the old Dowager to try to discover her side of the story. It might be difficult. And perhaps half an hour with Isabel Burton with her feisty determination to lead her life in her own way and not in the way her mother determined. And I would enjoy a walk around the estate with John, listening to his plans for the future.

Finally, the persecution of the Catholic minority that runs through this story like a dark thread . . . Anyone who has lived through most of the 20th century or studied its history, must believe that there is nothing more to be said or discovered about the story of persecution in Christian Europe. But it comes as a shock to encounter in the history of this country the sort of low-level religious persecution inflicted on the Arundells and their fellow Catholics over long years. It is as if we have a sort of national amnesia for certain unpalatable things. No doubt the excuse, then as now, was national security. The Spanish, the French, the Jacobites were enemies waiting to take over the country with the help of enemies within, weren't they? You cannot trust anyone who is different from the majority. What nonsense. There is no better way to build a strong, secure country than to make every citizen feel included and integrated and equally respected. The Penal Laws had exactly the opposite effect and the courage and loyalty of all those who suffered under them needs to be recognised. We live in an age of official apologies for past mistakes. Perhaps this apology is long overdue.

Notes

1 Thomas The Founder

1 There is no reliable date for his birth but it is believed to be about 1500.
2 They were described in William Lake's *A Complete Parochial History of the County of Cornwall*, 1867 as 'The Great Arundells; and greatest stroke, for love, living and respect in the Countrey heretofore they bare.'
3 His early dates are not precisely known but he was ordained in 1498 and became master of the school in the same year. The school was founded in 1480.
4 Her name is often given as Eleanor (as in the DNB) but this is wrong. Her husband John Arundell made his will in April 1513 en route to France in the service of Henry VIII and he left legacies, 'for people to sing and pray for my soul and that of Elizabeth my late wife . . . ' Cornwall Record Office at AR 21/9 (with thanks to Alison Spence).
5 There is no reliable date for her death.
6 Officially he was the King's first half cousin once removed.
7 On 7 August 1485 with 2-3,000 men.
8 Cavendish, 51.
9 National Archives, Cal IV, 4441, 30 June 1528.
10 CRO, AR/25/5-15.

11 sersnet = thin silk, literally Saracen's cloth.
12 Thomas's father went with the King and was knighted by him for valour in the Battle of the Spurs.
13 Russell, 45.
14 Dr. Starkey has said that he would like to have asked permission to include the chasuble in his exhibition on Henry VIII if he had known of its existence. 'It would have been a star exhibit.' (Henry VIII – Man and Monarch at the British Library, April to September 2009).
15 On the orphrey on the back of the chasuble are, from the bottom, Christ washing the disciples' feet, the Agony in the Garden, the Betrayal with, on the left, the arms of the Duke of Burgundy with the collar of the Golden Fleece and on the right, the arms of the Duke of Burgundy impaling the royal arms of England.
16 There is no documentation about the connection of the chasuble with Wardour. The 8th Lord brought a collection of vestments in Italy for the new chapel in the 1770s and 1780s but this was obviously not one of them.
17 Letters and Papers, vol IV, part III, 2577, ref. 5774.
18 Cavendish, 114.
19 Letters and Papers, vol IV, part III,

2783, ref. 6204, letter from Wolsey to Thomas Cromwell, February 1530.

20 Cavendish, 141.

21 National Archives, SP 158/6688 Pt.IV.

22 Still in existence and described by N. Pevsner in his *Buildings of England* series as 'too restored and altered to make a statement of any historical clarity.'

23 His father gave him twelve manors in Dorset as a wedding gift.

24 Wriothesley, 19.

25 Wiltshire and Swindon History Centre (WSHC): 2667/3/4.

26 Calendar of State Papers Spanish , vol IX p. 470.

27 Hayward, 148.

28 Nichols, Mackyn's Diary, 15.

2 Thomas The Valiant

1 George Gower was sergeant-painter to Elizabeth I from 1581. The Wardour Van Dyck is not listed in Susan Barnes et al: *Van Dyck, A Complete Catalogue of the Paintings*, Yale 2004.

2 Probably 1559 or maybe 1558. All the reference books give 1560 but they are not correct. See letter in *Salisbury Calendar*, July 1596, Thomas Arundell to Robert Cecil: 'And if in this I shew more passion than Aristotle doth allow to seven and thirty years of age . . .'

3 Lunn, 214.

4 Oliver, 77.

5 'Consanguineus noster perdilectus'.

6 *Salisbury Calendar*, 1606, Lord Arundell to the earl of Salisbury, 'In my first travels I was persuaded by the Duke of Guyse that then was, to offer my services to his Majesty's mother, which I did, yet with a reservation of my allegiance to our late Queen.' He explains that a letter about this was intercepted by Sir Francis Walsingham, 'whereupon I was banished from Court for thirteen months' and endured the Queen's displeasure.

7 Lunn, 131, 'their founding fathers had been partners in the crime of the century'.

8 *Salisbury Calendar*, 23 June 1597.

9 Lunn, 120.

10 '. . . and I do further swear that I do from my heart abhor, detest and abjure as impious and heretical this damnable doctrine and position that princes which be excommunicated by the Pope may be deposed or murdered by their subjects . . . .' Information about the 1st Lord's decision to take the Oath is in a box of the 10th Lord's notes, WSHC, 2667/24/1-2.

11 The source, no doubt, of one of the most ludicrously xenophobic comments in Europe recently; the Dutch EU Commissioner, Fritz Bokelstein said, 'Turkey's entry into the Union would mean that the defence of Vienna would have been in vain.'

12 See Shakespeare's *Othello*, Act 5, Scene 2.
'. . . Set you down this,
And say besides that in Aleppo once,
Where a malignant and a turbaned Turk
Beat a Venetian and traduced the state,
I took by th' throat the circumcised dog
And smote him thus.'
(He stabs himself)

13 *Calendar of State Papers in the Archives of Simancas* , vol II 1568-1579, 705-706.

14 The material for England's relations with the Ottoman Empire comes from articles by Pears (1893), Rawlinson (1923), Baumer (1944) and Wernham (1987).

15 Thomas Arundell's version of his

exploits is given in Webb, 1916.

16 Undoubtedly there is an account of the battle in the Turkish archives in Istanbul but it has not been located yet. Their version would be interesting.

17 A recent account of the opening of the Arundell crypt in St. John's Church, Tisbury in 1974 states that the helmet was found there amongst the coffins.

18 WSHC 2667/22/3/3.

19 Camden's version is in *Annalium rerum Anglicarium et Hibernicarum, Regnante Elizabetha*, vol III, A.D. 1717.

20 Professor John Guy says that the words were never used together unless there was a family relationship but the details have not been discovered.

21 All the letters can be found in the *Salisbury Calendar* between 1 February 1596 and 26 December 1598.

22 The Family History by Webb says he was shipwrecked off the Suffolk coast but this letter is from Ivybridge in Devon.

23 strangurye = slow and painful urination due to a blockage of the bladder.

24 WSHC 2667/8/84.

25 It is not known for how long this legacy was administered and distributed.

26 WSHC 2667/22/2/1.

27 In 2009 the Victoria and Albert Museum in London recreated a porcelain room in one of the cases in the World Ceramics Gallery (Room 145). This shows something of what must have been at Wardour.

28 See the article by Rodwell for a careful analysis of the building.

29 WSHC 2667/2/15.

30 In a letter of 1606 he reminded Cecil (*Salisbury Calendar*) 'Immediately on the death of our late Queen, I caused King James to be proclaimed in Shaftesbury on a market day, eight days before any neighbour town dust do the like.'

31 *Calendar of State papers Domestic, James I 1603-1610*, 246, the Tower.

32 *Salisbury Calendar*, 6 July 1607: 'The departure from this life of my dearest wife has so distressed my mind I cannot think of any other thing than of the greatness of my loss.'

33 To Anne Philipson of Westmoreland.

34 Life at Wardour was not completely peaceful before the Civil War. In November 1625 the King ordered Papists' houses to be searched for weapons and three cartloads were removed from Wardour (64 corseletts, 2 muskets, 7 lances, 44 staves for pikes, 7 petternells and 3 bucklers).

3 To Be A Catholic

1 *Calendar of Salisbury Manuscripts Part VII*, 167; a page of notes by Thomas Arundell about ships and guns is endorsed by Robert Cecil, 'This paper was found in Mr. Arundell his chamber the 30 April '97'; also a paper in Italian on the state of England was found in Arundell's house and endorsed by Cecil, 'this writing was left with the woman that kept Mr. Thomas Arundell's house the day and hour in which time he was examined by the Earl of Essex, The Lord Admiral and the Secretary.' Thomas wrote to Cecil, his kinsman on 9 May 1597, 'from my closest imprisonment', asking Cecil to entreat for his 'Liberty which would be dear unto me.'

2 WSHC 2667/3/3.

3 There has been much argument over whether the Bull was activated or merely published but it is surely a

sterile argument since its effect was catastrophic.

4   In March 1569 Pope Pius V consulted the Duke of Alva, Philip II's military commander in the Netherlands on the possibility of a joint Spanish/ French invasion of England but the Spanish were reluctant as they feared that Elizabeth's successor, Mary Queen of Scots would ally with France.

5   In the 1950s my mother frequently asked Anglican clergymen why the Arundells were buried in Tisbury church. None of them knew.

6   The boxes of papers are in WSHC 2667/25/1-3.

7   WSHC 2772/6.

8   Encyclical Letter, 19 January 1791 from the Vicars Apostolic of the Western, Northern and Southern Districts: 'None of the Faithful Clergy or Laity ought to take any new Oath.....without the previous approbation of their respective Bishop. The altered oath has not been approved by us and some recent publications are insulting to the Supreme Head of the Church . . .' in WSHC 2667/25/2/.

9   The crypt in the church was opened in 1974 and the collection of lead coffins was photographed; there were eight or nine including one of a baby, presumably the 8th Lord's daughter Anna Maria who died in 1771 aged one year and four months.

10 The chapels have all been closed; Donhead in 1959 and Ansty in 1962.

11 VCH vol III, 92-98 and vol XIII, 243-244.

4 Maryland

1   For example, in *Calendar of Manuscripts of the Marquis of Salisbury, Part VI*, 128, March 1596.

'My intention is to the East Indies where there are many kings so great ... . . . I will no doubt to conclude such an amity and intercourse of traffic as shall much weaken the Spanish strength in those parts and shall much enrich our merchants and by consequence the Queen . . . '

2   Born at Kiplin in Yorkshire where he bought the Hall in 1619 and rebuilt it from 1622 to 1625. It is open to the public and has an exhibition about the Calverts and Maryland.

3   The oath was passed by Parliament in May 1606. It was particularly difficult for Catholics to affirm that papal deposing power was heretical e.g. 'I do further swear that I do from my heart abhor, detest and abjure as impious and heretical this damnable doctrine . . . that princes may be excommunicated by the Pope . . . '

4   Named after the legendary place where crops grew untended, apple trees sprang from the grass and people lived to be over 100 years old.

5   There is confusion over Anne's dates; her tomb gives her age as 33 when she died in 1649 but that would mean she was 12 or 13 when she married in 1628. Her parents were married in 1608.

6   There may have been a small farmhouse on the site and it was re-built from 1635 to 1637. It was known as Baltimore House until the 1930s when the name was changed to Hook Manor. The 1st Lord Arundell appears to have given great financial help to the young couple as much of their money had gone to the new colony.

7   In the centre of the monogram panel are two doves eating a bunch of grapes.

8   The 1649 Maryland Act of Toleration was a landmark in the fight for religious toleration.

9 Again in March 1642 Thomas Gerard was fined the same amount for banning Protestants from using Maryland chapel for their services; he had removed the keys and destroyed their books. The Calverts said the chapel was to be used by Protestants and Catholics together.

10 Schismatick: a Catholic by conviction who conformed externally to the state religion.

11 Antinomian: a follower of a German sect which maintained that the moral law was not binding on Christians blessed by grace.

12 Barrowist: a follower of Henry Barrowe, founder of Congregationalism who was executed in 1593 for non- compliance with government rules.

13 Brownist: a follower of Robert Brown, an English Puritan.

14 Anna Arundelia Pulcherima et optima coniux caecilii Calverti;

I am greatly indebted to Professor John Krugler for the material in this chapter.

5 Lady Blanche and Civil War

1 Professor Ron Hutton considers that the Civil War was 'the bloodiest war this country has ever been engaged in, even including the Great War.' Out of a population of perhaps 4 million in England, there were 85,000 dead in the fighting, 90,000 wounded, 100,000 dead of diseases from involvement in the fighting and 55,000 homeless. There were 653 battles, skirmishes and sieges in the period 1642-1646.

2 S.R. Gardiner, *The History of the Great Civil War*, 1893, vol I, 167-68.

3 On 30 April 1643 the house and stables were attacked and plundered.

4 The Library of Corpus Christi College in Oxford holds original copies from May 1643 to March 1644. The British Library has a 1685 reprint of Mercurius or *The Countries Complaint of the barbarous Outrages committed by the Sectaries from the beginning of this Unnatural War to 25th March 1646* and this includes a small engraving of the siege of Wardour Castle.

5 It is perhaps surprising that Father Caraman SJ printed this account in his *The Years of Siege: Catholic Life from James I to Cromwell*, 1966, Longmans, without any comment or warning.

6 Lady Blanche Arundell, sixth daughter of the 4th earl of Worcester of Raglan Castle. Her father was Master of the Horse and a close friend of King James I. He took the Oath of Allegiance and married a Catholic who brought up the eleven children as Catholics. Lady Blanche eloped to marry Thomas Arundell in 1607. The King disapproved of the marriage but Cecil reported 'they have clapped up the marriage privately.'

7 Luke Hughes has found a cannon ball in his garden at Wardour House next to the south bailey wall.

8 Quarter means the exemption from being immediately put to death, granted to a defeated opponent in a battle or siege.

9 This was presumably the original source for the famous Victorian painting reproduced in Cattermole's History.

10 A meeting with the enemy, under terms of truce, for discussion of surrender details.

11 Pieces have been found during excavations and a reconstruction drawn by Peter Dunn (*Country Life*, 10 February 1971).

12 The implication is clearly that this theological and political condition was

as dangerous as the medical infection in Bath.

13 WSHC 2667/22/4/1.

14 A large portable gun supported on a tripod.

15 Sir Francis Doddington: a prominent Somerset Royalist with a reputation for cruelty. In June 1644, he ordered the hanging near Horningsham in Wiltshire of fourteen men he had captured at Wardour.

16 This appears to be a contradiction but wheel-locks had such a complicated mechanism that if they were left wound up for more than a few hours they frequently jammed. (information from Dr. John Wroughton).

6 Politics, Power and Plots

1 The battle of Stratton took place a few miles inland from Bude, on 16 May 1643 when Sir Ralph Hopton defeated the Parliamentary forces of Lord Stamford. Hopton had half the number of men on the enemy side and he took 1,700 prisoners. The 2nd Lord Arundell died at Oxford on 19 May.

2 *The Letters of Dorothy Osborne to Sir William Temple, 1652-54*, 1888 edited by E.A. Parry, 87.

3 It has never been clear why the Arundells rented Breamore for over 100 years. They had extensive estates in Hampshire.

4 *A History of the Early Part of the Reign of James the Second*, 1808, 23.

5 *Burnet's History*, vol I, 166.

6 Uglow, 371.

7 A copy of the secret Treaty of Dover was found a few years ago by Professor Ron Hutton in Lord Clifford's attic at Ugbrooke.

8 Titus Oates (1649-1705); a superb actor and pathological liar. He joined the Navy in 1675 as a chaplain but was expelled in 1676 for homosexual practices.

9 Father Manuel de Calatayud from the English College at Valladolid where Oates studied in June 1677, later wrote: 'He was a curse. What I went through and suffered from that man, God alone knows.' (DNB).

10 WSHC: 2667/25/1.

11 In 1673 when Oates was curate to his father the vicar of Hastings, he accused the local schoolmaster of sodomy with one of his pupils in the church porch, simply because he wanted the master's job. The story was a complete fabrication and Oates was put on trial for perjury but did not turn up in court.

12 For example, written at the back of a notebook used for everyday business (WSHC, 2667/12/37), such poems as: *A Consideration Upon Death, Of the Benefit of the Resignation to God's Will, A Valediction to the World.*

7 Good Marriages

1 Walpole is generally known as Britain's first prime minister c. 1720 to 1742.

2 For example, his third son Horace was made, for life: usher of the exchequer, comptroller of the pipe and clerk of the estreates, all bringing in a good income without any work.

3 An obsolete gambling game in which the players bet on the order in which certain cards will appear when taken singly from the top of the pack.

4 Moll Davis (1651-1718), an actress whose legs Pepys described as 'very fine'. When Moll became Charles II's mistress, Nell Gwyn was so jealous that she put a laxative in her drink on the evening before she spent the night with the King. The laxative worked but the plan did not because

the King was besotted with her. She gave birth in 1673 to the 17th and last of the King's 'official' bastards, a daughter, Mary.

5 The reason they gave was 'concerns about health' but presumably it was for religious reasons.

6 Sold from the Wardour Castle collection in 1995.

7 The *Estates Gazette* of 3 July 1915 commented, 'a price of this magnitude in war time is a remarkable testimony to British confidence.'

8 Pimp.

9 WSHC 2667/20/14 to 20.

10 A method of protecting wall fruit trees by building over-hanging projections.

11 Probably the marriage of the 7th Lord's brother to Mary Porter. There were no children and he died in 1768.

12 Wrights were London bankers where the Arundells had an account; eventually part of the Nat West Bank.

13 Uncle Everard lived at Arundells in The Close Salisbury which came to him with Ashcombe from his marriage to the heiress Anne Wyndham in 1751. Unfortunately Arundells is now a self-created memorial to Edward Heath.

14 This perhaps indicates better than anything else that the Arundells made only short visits to Wardour after the destruction of the old castle.

15 Probably Uncle Everard and his brother Raymond.

16 Ashcombe was in a remote valley on the Downs in Berwick St. John. It was the home of Cecil Beaton in the 1930s and 1940s and recently belonged to the singer, Madonna.

17 A Catholic landowner had to register his estates with the magistrates when he inherited them according to the statute I George I, occasioned by the Jacobite rebellion of 1715.

18 George III was crowned in Westminster Abbey on 22 September 1761.

19 WSHC 2667/12/150.

20 Laura Arundell was described by Lady Jerringham in 1786 as 'tall and pretty but has that same gawky stoop that she had when she was a girl.'

21 Dr. Venner, *Via Recta ad Vitam Longam*, 1638.

22 Embroidery applied by using a frame.

23 The large expenditure on shoes for Laura may have been due to preparations for her marriage on 29 November 1786 to Lord Clifford's brother and heir.

8 Henry the Magnificent

1 There were six Catholic families: Arundell, Clifford, Dormer, Petre, Shrewsbury and Stourton.

2 Window tax on Old Wardour House in 1796 was for 15 windows and for the new castle, for 150. WSHC, 2667/12/154.

3 It is perhaps unfair to wish that he had had the imagination to spend some of his vast resources on philanthropic schemes such as those of Thomas Coram, the London merchant (1668-1751) who set up the famous Foundling Hospital in 1739, 'motivated by an enduring blend of Christian benevolence, practical morality and civic spirit.' Henry made generous donations to the Church.

4 Professor Habakkuk has commented, 'The age of the great house is now so remote that it is natural for us to wonder why men employed so much wealth building them.'

5 His younger brother Thomas had great financial problems. 46 letters survive from 1770 when his brother Henry and Uncle Everard of The

Close in Salisbury tried to help him, without success. He had debts of £4,512.3.6 ¼ in May 1770, of which the biggest item was £1,516.16.2 ½ 'to Innes'. He spent a great deal of time 'sodine at ye Kings Arms' in London.

6   Stuart McKenzie, second son of the earl of Bute who was British envoy in Turin, 1758-1760.

7   Giles Hussey (1710-1788), a member of a Catholic family of Nash Court, Marnhull, Dorset who was famous for his profile heads.

8   Oliver, 88.

9   WSHC 2667/12/151 and Lady Arundell's Household Accounts are at 2667/12/150.

10 It is very difficult to calculate acres but notes made by an agent in a small book at the time of the sales to pay creditors, c. 1804, have been very helpful, WSHC 2667/12/222. For the Cornish estates see Cornwall Record Office, AR/8/146.

11 The East India Company was about to sign a contract for the supply of Cornish tin to China where it was needed for religious ceremonies.

12 see Parker.

13 They eventually produced a 78 page Deed of Arrangement with Creditors, 27 May 1802. WSHC 2667/22/Box 8.

14 James Everard Arundell, later to be 9th Lord and the 6th Lord Clifford.

15 WSHC 2667/20/Files 19-24.

16 For example the Grosvenor debts led to the trustees developing Mayfair with great energy, 1789-1800.

17 Knight's letters are at 2667/20/Box 6/File 4.

18 Henry's marriage settlement of 20 May 1763 explains the position: 'Henry, seized as Tenant in tail in Possession with remainder to his Brother and Uncles and their Male Issue has barred such Estate Tail and gained to himself a good present Estate of Freehold in Fee Simple . . . and being further seized of an Estate in Remainder immediately expectant on the decease of his mother.'

19 Lord Arundell's Account Book for work on the new castle, WSHC 2667/12/29.

20 A Dutch visitor in 1791 believed the building costs exceeded £200,000 but that may have included fittings and furnishings.

21 The cost of furnishing Harewood House in Yorkshire with pieces by Chippendale the elder was £10,000.

22 WSHC 2667/20/22/1-12.

23 William Bankes (1786-1855), Dorset Record Office, D/BKL to Mary Bankes, 1811.

24 Alderman William Beckford left the 4,900 acre Fonthill estate to his son William who began to build the new abbey in 1796.

25 The mile post at the top of White Sheet Hill says 97 miles to Hyde Park Corner.

26 Beckett, 200.

9 *Wardour the Magnificent*

1   Horace Walpole: *Journals*, 6 February 1783.

2   WSHC 2667/20/Box 1.

3   WSHC 2667/21/13.

4   Our knowledge of Richard Woods owes a great deal to the research of Fiona Cowell; see her articles on Woods.

5   WSHC 2667/20/Box 2.

6   WSHC 2667/21/10.

7   There is controversy about the making of this terrace. Woods uses the word 'Terrafs' to refer to various schemes including 'the great Terafs' by Bridzor Field which presumably meant the platform for the new house, since he built 42 rods of ha ha ditch around it. But there is no doubt

that Woods was partly responsible for the terrace on the hillside too, e.g. 15 March 1766, 'To making the new Terrafs or Shais road from the Castle garden to Lady Grove, is already done.' The 10th Lord may have completed the hillside terrace.

8   John Britton.

9   The colossal Fonthill Abbey built by William Beckford (1760-1844), 'England's wealthiest son' with an annual income of £155,000 a year from slave plantations. He began to build the abbey in 1796 and the tower collapsed in 1825. He was as reclusive as the Arundells were gregarious.

10 This is a mystery as to origin and purpose and may have been built by the 10th Lord in the 1820s.

11 The temple was given by the Jesuits to Mrs. Cowell in the 1980s and moved by her to the garden of Hatfield Priory in Essex.

12 The ice house was 500 m. from the nearest pond, an important consideration. It was demolished in the 1980s, leaving only eighteen intact in Wiltshire.

13 The popularity of bathing in cold water in the 18th century owes a great deal to John Floyer's book published in 1700, *The History of Cold Bathing*. He pointed out that the success of the Roman Empire owed much to their use of cold baths.

14 The Cold Bath was incorporated into Ark Farm. One of the best examples of a Cold Bath is the one formerly at Arno's Court, Brislington, Bristol and moved to Portmeirion in 1950 by Clough Williams-Ellis.

15 The Wardour camellias are very famous since the plants there may be the oldest Alba Plenas known to be growing anywhere in the world. They were producing flowers for sale in Covent Garden as late as the 1960s.

Japanese tourists regularly visit the Wardour Camellia House.

16 Pevsner, *The Buildings of England, Wiltshire*, 552.

17 WSHC 2667/20/Box 2.

18 WSHC 2667/20/22/1-12.

19 It is clear that Lord Arundell was reluctant to display any paintings showing naked bodies. Thorpe found this strange and peculiarly English.

20 Now on the ceiling of the Music Room.

21 Richard Warner: *Excursions from Bath*, 1801.

22 The Vernets are in the J. Paul Getty Museum in Los Angeles; the Titian of St. Bernardine is in the National Gallery in London and the Batoni in the National Gallery in Rome.

10 'Trying To Pay Grandfather's Bills'

1   Habakkuk, 328.

2   James Morrison (1789-1857), an orphan from Middle Wallop who made a fortune in London as a wholesale haberdasher; friend of Francis Place, Robert Owen and other radicals. He bought the Fonthill estate from George Mortimer and when he died left £6 million (£500 million in 2010 values) and 100,000 acres. He is greatly in need of a biographer.

3   When he died his wife was heart-broken but remarked to friends that one consolation was that she would be able to reach decisions without days of discussion and delay.

4   The 9th Duke was weak-willed, selfish and extravagant. He left debts of £500,000 when he died in 1839.

5   The transport of the books from Wardour to Stonyhurst took three months in 1837 and consisted of: cart to Salisbury; packed in cases there and by cart to Bristol; ship to Liverpool; canal barge to Manchester;

cart to Enfield near the college.

6 Habakkuk, 309.

7 See DNB.

8 The gold pocket watch that belonged to Fox may have come to the Arundells via this connection.

9 The money for his books came mainly from a government sinecure, chief justice on eyre south of the Trent, given him as a child and producing £2,000 a year.

10 He was notorious for meanness e.g. when he left office he took with him boxes of official pens, ink and stationery.

11 For an account of Blackie's career see Parker.

12 Jeffrey's survey in 1851 was the first since Ingman's in 1768, WSHC 2667/12/239. He later complained bitterly that he was not rewarded adequately for all the work he did, 2667/11/216.

13 WSHC 2667/20/51.

14 WSHC 2667/20/52.

15 WSHC 2667/20/55.

16 WSHC 2667/20/57.

17 Earl Grosvenor (1795-1891) bought the Fonthill Abbey estate in 1844. He hated extravagance and ostentation.

18 Mr. Mortimer was a nephew of John Farquhar, a gunpowder millionaire who bought the whole Beckford estate in 1823; Farquhar sold the Abbey portion to the Benetts of Pythouse who sold it on to Earl Grosvenor and he gave the Fonthill portion to his nephew in 1826. WSHC 2667/20/50.

19 Place Farm was a grange of Shaftesbury Abbey and is one of the most impressive survivals of Abbey property with its 61 m. longbarn and 14th century farmhouse, used by the abbess as a country retreat It came to the Arundells in 1541.

20 WSHC 2667/20/59.

21 WSHC 2667/20/59/2.

22 WSHC 2667/20/60.

11 'A Wild, Roving, Vagabond Life'

1 This story and references to their early meetings come from Burton vol I, 166. The letter to Isabel's mother is on p.332.

2 Lady Hester Stanhope (1776-1839), niece of Pitt the Younger and great traveller in the Middle East where she wore male Turkish clothes; she spent nearly 30 years in Syria and Lebanon.

3 Beginning with *Goa and the Blue Mountains* and ending with *Falconry in the Valley of the Indus*.

4 If a photograph taken after 1854 shows Burton looking to the left and without a scar on his cheek it was taken on his right side and wrongly printed.

5 This was one of the great unsolved questions. The expedition was also supported by the Foreign Office and the East India Company which indicates that the political and economic issues were recognised.

6 John Speke (1827-1854) was a great explorer who led a second expedition in September 1860 and found the place where the Nile issues from Lake Victoria. His quarrel with Burton was ended when he died in a shooting accident at Neston Park near Corsham on 15 September 1864.

7 For example *The Mountains of the Moon*, made in 1989 with Patrick Bergin as Burton.

8 The importance of country houses in the life of Victorian Society is indicated by this comment.

9 Isabel's mother was very proud that she belonged to the Gerard family, an old-established Catholic family, family. Her brother was the 1st Lord Gerard.

10 Cardinal Wiseman (1802-1865), first

cardinal archbishop of Westminster; he organised the restoration of the Catholic hierarchy in England and welcomed converts from the Anglican church.

11 WSHC 2667/26/Box 3.

12 In 2009 in Khajuraho, you could choose from, *The Idiot's Guide to the Kama Sutra, The Pop-up Kama Sutra, The Office Kama Sutra* or Burton's translation which was the most expensive because it was 'authentic'.

13 Kennedy, 227.

14 Kennedy, 206.

15 W.G. Archer was an ICS officer in India between the wars and a great scholar.

16 *A Wiltshire Childhood*, privately printed 1993, 3.

17 In 2010 there is an appeal for £50,000 to restore the building in St Mary's churchyard, Mortlake.

12 *The Disastrous Dowager*

1 When I interviewed Mrs. Eva Morgan (1903-1982), a member of the long-established Foyle family at Wardour, in 1981 she was anxious to record the kindness of the old Dowager in providing a cottage on the estate for her and her husband when they married in 1928.

2 WSHC 2667/24/1/3B.

3 Trading in small amounts like a pedlar or hawker.

4 Cecil Turner was a generous benefactor of Wardour and paid for restoration work and the cleaning of pictures in the 1930s.

5 Major sales were held on 6, 13 and 14 June 1935, including dozens of pictures.

6 John's 21st birthday was celebrated in July 1928 with a party for 500 tenants and friends at the castle but the old Dowager declined to attend it.

7 Williamson, *Wardour and the Arundells*, 10. Martina evoked brilliantly the Wardour of another age.

8 WSHC 2667/22/53 and plan of the estate at 2667/11/279.

9 WSHC 2667/17/14.

10 The demand by Irish nationalists for independence for Ireland, led by Charles Stewart Parnell from 1881. Gladstone introduced the first Home Rule Bill in 1886 and his second Bill was defeated in the House of Lords in 1893.

11 Harcourt was Liberal Chancellor of the Exchequer from 1892 to 1895 and introduced Death Duties in his 1894 Budget with the claim, 'We are all Socialists now.'

12 The Church of the Sacred Heart opened on 3 November 1898.

13 *The Letters of Rudyard Kipling*, vo.2, 1890-99, edited by T. Pinney, Macmillan 1990; letter to Henry James.

14 Visitors Books for the new Castle, WSHC 2667/22/2/11, for 1844 to 1902.

15 WSHC 2667/22/2/12, Visitors Book For the Old Castle 1879-1904.

16 The codicils listed all the 22 potential heirs to Wardour if the main male line became extinct – Talbots, Wickhams, Radcliffes, Welds, Van Zellers, Mostyns, O'Kellys and Pigott-Smyths. The 12th Lord must have had an encyclopaedic knowledge of his relatives. WSHC 2667/8/8.

17 The will was signed on 8 February 1905, Gerald married Ivy Segrave on 9 January 1906, the 12th Lord died on 26 October 1906 and John, Gerald and Ivy's son was born on 18 June 1907.

18 A similar arrangement caused havoc with the Blathwayt estate at Dyrham in Gloucestershire. A late 19th

century squire made a will settlement stipulating that if a Catholic should ever inherit the estate, the inheritance would be barred. When Christopher Blathwayt, a Catholic, inherited in 1936 he had to hand over the estate to his brother and the will was only altered, eventually, at vast expense by the House of Lords.

19 WSHC 2667/8/8 and 2667/22/2/8.
20 *A Wiltshire Childhood* privately printed in 1993,6.
21 WSHC 2667/20/124.
22 WSHC 2667/20/94.
23 WSHC 2667/12/242.
24 WSHC 2667/20/94.

13 *Family Life at Wardour*

1 Ivy Florence Mary, daughter of Capt. W. Segrave; she met Gerald while on a visit to Wardour.
2 A sport in which horsemen with sword or lance gallop to pierce, pick up and carry away small ground targets, representing tent pegs.
3 Williamson: *Wardour and the Arundells*, 11.
4 Her pay was '5 shillings a week and any tips from visitors. We were allowed one half day off a week. I had to be back by 9.30 or 10.00. If we wanted to go to Salisbury – it was a big treat – we had to ask permission so we could leave before lunch.'.
5 The 13th Duke (1862-1940), a sailor, succeeded his cousin in 1895; he spent a great deal of time at Ferne. His wife Nina (1878-1951) founded the Scottish Society for the Prevention of Vivisection and set up the animal sanctuary at Ferne.
6 David Lloyd George (1863-1945): a great social reformer and the Prime Minister who 'won the War'; he taxed the super rich for the benefit of the poor, introducing Old Age Pensions

and National Insurance. He imposed three new land taxes and described the House of Lords as 'no more than 500 ordinary men chosen at random from amongst the unemployed.'
7 *The Salisbury Journal*, July 1928.
8 A.L. d'Abreu (1916-1924, at Stonyhurst) in *The Stonyhurst Magazine* July 1954.
9 Tom Burns (1922-1925) in the *Stonyhurst Magazine*, Autumn 1991.
10 Goronwy Rees in Buxton and Williams, 121 and 124.
11 Dick Crossman (1907-1974), educated at Winchester and New College, Left wing Labour M.P.; Douglas Jay (1907-1996), educated at Winchester and New College, Labour M.P. for nearly 40 years, opposed to UK entry to the EC.

14 *Wardour in Wartime*

1 From his Army Service File.
2 Williamson, *Wardour and the Arundells*, 17.
3 The names of all the camps are recorded in the Red Cross archives in Geneva, 074.4 3901 GB/mfg.
4 A.N.L. Munby (1913-1974) was Librarian of King's College, Cambridge. He was in German prison camps from 1940 to 1945 with John. His papers and those of Brigadier Robert Loder, another fellow prisoner, are in the college Library.
5 Lord Beveridge (1879-1963), social reformer, educated at Balliol College Oxford; he was fired with a mission for social justice and wrote the reports that were the inspiration for the Welfare State. He was one of the giants of 20th century Britain.
6 Bence-Jones, *The Catholic Families*, 303.
7 Archives of the Sisters of Nazareth, Hammersmith Rd, London W6 8DB.

8   John Savage and Larry Barnett have been very helpful too.

9   Presumably in the stable yard attached to the east wing and demolished in the 1960s.

10 This is a mystery. We know he wrote letters to the Agent as they are referred to in the Agent's replies and there must have been letters to the family.

11 J.E.R. Wood, *Detour*, The Falcon Press 1946, 69.

12 Archives du CICR, Geneva. ACICR/C/SC Allemagne, WKIV/VII RT.

13 Hopetoun was the son of the marquess of Linlithgow, viceroy of India 1936-1943; Alexander was the son of the British commander, Field Marshal Alexander; Romilly was a journalist who had fought the Fascists in Spain and was Lady Churchill's nephew. These men were kept as special prisoners so they could be used as hostages if Germany faced defeat.

14 Letters from Lt.Cdr. J.M. Moran and J. Hamilton-Baillie in WSHC 2776/7

15 WSHC 2667/20/128.

16 Duggan, 231.

17 Sir Martin Gilliat (1913-1993), army officer and landowner; he was a prisoner from 1940 to 1945, escaping four times; private secretary to the Queen Mother 1956-1993 and dispenser of 'fortifying drinks' for her guests.

18 WSHC 2772/7.

19 His name is recorded on the War memorial in Tisbury Square along with fourteen comrades who also died.

20 WSHC 2772/6.

Additional Notes

The Value of Money

THE Bank of England publishes a table of contemporary values of the pound, showing how the value of money has changed over the past seven centuries. Thus £95.57 would have been required in January 2007 in order to have the same purchasing power as £1 in 1690; £325.48 in 2007 was equivalent to £1 in 1540 and so on. It is tempting to convert all sums of money in this account to modern equivalents but that would be tedious, so only a few have been done. Also it should be remembered that the conversion table takes no account of the changing values of goods within a period in the past e.g. a small family home is now worth much more relatively than 500 years ago.

Films

WARDOUR has been used for at least three films in recent times. *Robin Hood, Prince of Thieves* was issued in July 1991 and starred Kevin Costner as Robin Hood. The old castle was used as the ancestral home of Robin's father who rode to his death through the main castle gate when the masked sheriff of Nottingham arrived. The film was nominated for an Oscar. The new castle was the setting for the audition scenes at the Royal Ballet School in *Billy Elliot*, produced in 2000 and starring Jamie Ball as the eleven year old Billy. The film won many awards. The lakes at Wardour were used in *Chocolat* issued in 2001. Directed by Lasse Hallstorm, the film was nominated for five Oscars.

Excavations at Wardour

THE old castle was placed in the guardianship of the Ministry of Works on 13 July 1936, national monument number 26706. A large-scale archaeological excavation is long overdue at Wardour. There were minor excavations in 1938, 1962, 1965 and 1990. Reports on excavations at Wardour have appeared in the Wiltshire Archaeological and Natural History Magazine, vol. 62 (1967) and vol. 80 (1985). The English Heritage store at Fort Brockhurst at Gosport near Portsmouth holds 112 objects found at the old castle. They range from the limestone finial of a lion's head to window glass, clay pipes, a horseshoe, a brooch, a shaving stick and a marble head. It would be good to think that these might be displayed one day in a museum at Wardour.

Major Sales

June 1900: the four portraits by Reynolds, sold to Messers Robinson for 11,000 gns.

June 1935: 200 pictures (including works by Mytens, Vernet, Breughal, Salvator Rosa), 1,200 books, china, furniture and jewellery, under instructions in the will of the Dowager Lady Arundell.

September 1946: 3,000 acres including 13 farms and 70 cottages for £78,000, sold by Messers J.D. Wood & Co.

1947: New Castle sold to the Jesuits.

3 and 4 June 1948: a two day sale of the contents of New Wardour Castle; furniture, wall mirrors, silver, paintings (works by Teniers, Wootton, Batoni), books and china.

September 1952: all the remaining contents of the castle except family portraits.

1961: New Castle sold to Cranborne Chase School.

1992: New Castle sold to Nigel Tuersley and converted to apartments.

8 June 1995: 47 family portraits removed from Wardour Castle and sold at Christie's in London. The highest price was £17,250 for Henry Howard, 6th Duke of Norfolk by John Michael Wright.

May 1998: a rare 19th century Ziegler carpet made for Wardour Castle sold by Woolley and Wallis for £94,600. The owner bought the carpet for a few pounds at the castle sale in 1948 and gave it to her dog to chew.

August 2010: Jasper Conran bought the central apartment at Wardour Castle. The *Daily Mail* reported, 'Fashion designer Jasper snaps up £7 million Billy Elliot house for just £2.75 million'.

Hillside Gardens

THERE used to be a cottage at the edge of the woods above the old castle, looking over Twelve Acre Copse towards Ansty Coombe. This was obviously not an ordinary cottage because it had two large Venetian windows and a grand central door between them, on the east side. Unfortunately the cottage has now been demolished. It was the last relic of the early 18th century walled garden laid out by the Arundells to provide food for the household at Old Wardour House. Stan Macey lived in the house with his parents from 1942 to 1944 and although the gardens had long disappeared, he remembers an old mulberry tree to the side of the house. The original plan of the garden is in the archives (WSHC 2667/21/14). Stan remembers that the house was quite remote and deliveries and post were left in Antsy Coombe. Before the war, there was a silver fox farm at the north east corner of the field.

The Cold Bath

ONE of the most interesting buildings at Wardour was the Cold Bath, erected by Richard Woods in 1766 (see Chapter 8). The Cold Bath, with its splendid portico, was converted to a two-roomed lodge in 1811

(WSHC 2667/22/4/2). The Cold Bath itself was filled in and became the kitchen with a new staircase to bedrooms added above. Edmund and Margaret Neville-Rolfe bought the house in 1951 and in 1958 enlarged it with a new drawing room which necessitated the removal of the portico. This was re-erected on the side of the building nearest the Swan Pond and remains as one of the most evocative survivals from the 18th century landscaping of the Park.

John Arundell's Prisons in Germany

23.5.1940:	captured at Roeux and made prisoner of war	
8.6.1940:	Transit Camp at Mainz	Dulag XII
6.7.1940:	Officers' Camp at Laufen	Oflag VII/C
11.11.1940:	Officers' Camp at Tittmoning	Oflag VII/C/Z
11.10.1941:	Dossel Camp	Oflag VI/B
12.9.1942:	Eichstatt Camp	Oflag VII/B
	(escaped and captured on 7.6.43)	
29.6.1943:	Colditz Camp	Oflag IV/C
18.4.1944:	Obermassfeld Military Hospital	—
–.5.1944:	Elsterhorst Military Hospital	Stalag IV/A
5.9.1944:	Military Hospital Train	Lzrt Zug No 114v2123
–.9.1944:	boarded ship at Goteborg for Liverpool	

(extracted from records in the Red Cross Archives, Geneva)

Foreign Titles and Decorations

ELIZABETH I's anger at Thomas Arundell's acceptance of the title of Count from the Holy Roman Emperor in 1595 has an echo 350 years later. Joseph Needham, the famous scientist and expert on Chinese culture was awarded the Order of the Brilliant Star by the Chinese government in October 1947. As a matter of courtesy he reported this to the British Foreign Office. They consulted King George VI who, despite the pressing burdens of kingship at a time of national economic emergency, took the matter very seriously. There was a long investigation of the issue. Nearly two years later, the King's Private Secretary, Sir Alan Lascelles, informed Needham that he was allowed to wear the Order but only in China and in the presence of Chinese officials. By then the Chinese Nationalist government had fled to Formosa so the matter was not greatly relevant. This is surely an example of the British Establishment at its most ludicrous.

A Comparison with the Neighbours

In 1876 John Bateman published a survey of the landowners of Great Britain and Ireland. He included all those who owned more than 2000 acres and more. In many cases the entries were corrected by the owners themselves. This table shows how greatly the Wardour estate had been damaged by the bankruptcy of the 8th Lord and how small it had become in comparison with other Wiltshire and Dorset landowners

Name	Total Acres	Acres in Wilts/Dorset	Total annual land income	House
Arundell	6,219	6,037	£9,174	Wardour
Pitt-Rivers	27,704	Same	£35,396	Rushmore
Pembroke	44,806	42,244	£77,720	Wilton
Salisbury	20,202	3,130	£33,413	Hatfield
Shaftesbury	21,785	18,535	£16,083	St. Giles
Ilchester	32,849	18,114	£43,452	Melbury
Benett	6,997	5,026	£25,306	Pyt
Morrison	8,184	Same	£6,571	Fonthill
Bath	55,574	19,984	£68,015	Longleat
Lansdowne	142,916	11,145	£62,025	Bowood

Anne Arundell's Tombstone in Tisbury Church

WHEN Anne Arundell died in 1649 she was buried in the Arundell family crypt in Tisbury church. Her husband, the second Lord Baltimore, composed a beautiful Latin inscription for her tombstone. It reads:

Phoenicis quicquid est

in

Floribus, Gemmis, Gratis

(ipsa in coelis quanta)

Hic iacet

ANNA ARUNDELIA DOMINA BALTEMOREA

Anagram

NON ALIA IN ORBE TAM REDAMANDA, VALE

Amoris ergo coniunx P.

Cessit humanis X Kalendas sextileis

Anno Aetat XXXIII Ab Infante deo

The Latin composition reflects the determination of Anne's husband to use the very best of his high-grade humanistic learning to show the world his love for his beautiful wife. A rough translation is:

Here lies Anne Arundell, Lady Baltimore

Epitome of all the qualities of the Phoenix

That there are in flowers, buds and graces

(those being as great as there are in Heaven)

Farewell: no other woman's love in the world was to be so requited.

She left this world on July 23rd in the 1649th year

From the childhood of God and the 34th year of her age.

This memorial was set up by her husband for his love's sake.

Several aspects of the inscription require comment. The word Anagram is simply a way for Cecil Calvert to point out that he has devised an anagram of the lines above and below the word (U and V were interchangeable). Anagrams were very popular in the early 17th century and this is a splendid example. Every letter in the top line is used again in the bottom. P stands for 'posuit', meaning 'he placed' or 'set up'

The most interesting aspect of the whole composition is the evidence it carries of the politics of 1649. On 30 January 1649 King Charles was beheaded. When Anne died in July, England was a Republic. Cecil Calvert may have wanted to curry favour with the new rulers. The evidence is the extraordinary way he has written the date in antique Republican Latin that was not in use at any time after AD 4. Anyone after that date would have written 'Augustas' for August but Cecil uses 'sextileis', the sixth month (the Romans began their year in March so the sixth month was August). Even more extraordinary is the spelling of 'sextileis', which was found only in early Republican inscriptions before about 100 BC. Most people between 100 BC and AD 4 would have written 'sextilis'.

All this may have been designed to avoid showing any Royalist sympathies in the early days of the English Republic and to flatter the new rulers. The threat that worried Calvert was that Parliament might take over his estates in Maryland, named after the ex Queen and populated by Catholics. His flattery did not work. In 1652 Parliament appointed Commissioners to rule the colony but eventually in 1658 Calvert's rights were restored.

(I am very grateful to David Miller, formerly Head of Classics at Bristol Grammar School for explaining the meaning of the inscription to me).

Bibliography

Archer, W.G., 1963: *The Kama Sutra of Vatsyayana*, George Allen and Unwin

Arundell J.E. and Hoare R.C., 1829: *The History of Modern Wiltshire*, London

Arundell, Lady, 1909: *Some Papers of Lord Arundell of Wardour*, Longman

Baldwin Smith, Lacey, 1961: *A Tudor Tragedy*, London

Bank of England, 2009: *Inflation Calculator*

Bateman, J., 1876: *The Great Landowners of Great Britain*, London

Beckett, J.V., 1986: *The Aristocracy in England 1660-1914*, Blackwell

Beckett, J.V., 1994: *The Rise and Fall of the Grenvilles*, Manchester University
Press

Bellenger, D.A., 1986: *The French Exiled Clergy in the British Isles*, Downside
Abbey

Bettey, J., 1993: *Estates and the English Countryside*, Batsford

Brady, J., Oberman H. and Tracy J., 1994: *A Handbook of European History 1400-
1600*, Michigan

Brewer, J.S., Gairdner, J. and Brodie, R., 1882: *Letters and Papers, Foreign and
Domestic of the Reign of Henry VIII*, London

Burton, Isabel, 1893: *The Life of Capt. Sir Richard Burton*, Chapman and Hall

Britton, J., 1801: *Beauties of Wiltshire*, vol. I, Salisbury

Calendar of State Papers Spanish, 1912. vol. IX and X, HMSO

Calendar of Manuscripts of the Marquis of Salisbury, 1883-1976, HMSO

Camden, William, 1717: *Annales rerum Anglicarum*, vol. III

Cannadine, J., 1990: *The Decline and Fall of the British Aristocracy*, Yale

Cannon, J., 1984: *Aristocratic Century, the Peerage of 18th century England*, CUP

Cannon, J. (ed), 1997: *The Oxford Companion to British History*, Oxford

Caraman, P., 1966: *The Years of Siege: Catholic Life from James I to Cromwell*, Longman

Cavendish, George, 1962: *The Life and Death of Cardinal Wolsey*, The Folio Society

Chandler, John, 2003: *A Higher Reality: the History of Shaftesbury Royal Nunnery*, The Hobnob Press

Coffin, D., 1994: *The English Garden*, Princeton

Cornwall, Julian, 1977: *The Revolt of the Peasantry 1549*, Routledge

Doran, Susan, 2000: *Elizabeth I and Foreign Policy 1558-1603*, Routledge

Doran, Susan, 1986: *England and Europe 1485-1603*, Longman

Doran, Susan and Starkey, David, 2009: *Henry VIII, Man and Monarch*, Catalogue for the British Library exhibition

Duggan, Mary, 1978: *Padre in Colditz, the Diary of Ellison Platt*, Hodder

Durres, Alan, 1983: *English Catholicism 1558-1642*, Longman

Eggers, R., 1972: *Colditz, The German Viewpoint*, New English Library

English, B. and Savile, J., 1983: *Strict Settlement: A Guide*, Hull U.P.

Firth C.H., 1894: *The Memoirs of Edmund Ludlow 1625-1672*, vol. I, Oxford

Foister, Susan, 2006: *Holbein in England*, Tate Gallery

Foley, Henry, 1878: *Records of the English Province of the Society of Jesus* vol.III, Burns and Oates

Fox H.A.S. and Padel O.J., 2000: *The Cornish Lands of the Arundells of Lanherne*, Exeter

Fraser, Antonia, 1996: *The Gunpowder Plot*, Weidenfeld

Girouard, M., 1966: *Robert Smythson and the Architecture of the Elizabethan Era*, Country Life

Girouard, M., 1980: *The English Country House*, Penguin

Green, V.H.H., 1952: *Renaissance and Reformation*, Edward Arnold

Guy, John, 1998: *Cardinal Wolsey*, Headstart History

Habakkuk, J., 1994: *Marriage, Debt and the Estates System*, Oxford

Hadfield, Miles, 1960: *Gardening in Britain*, Hutchinson

Hamilton Rogers, W.H., 1890: *The Strife of the Roses*, Exeter

Hayward, John, 1993: *The Life and Raigne of King Edward the Sixth*, Kent State

University Press

Hayward, Maria, 2007: *Dress at the Court of King Henry VIII*, Maney

Hughes, Pat, 2000: The *Building By The Pond*, Privately printed

Hutchinson, Robert, 2009: *House of Treason*, Weidenfeld

Hutton, Ronald, 1989: *Charles the Second*, Oxford

Hutton, Ronald, 1999: *The Royalist War Effort*, Routledge

Inalcik, Halil, 2000: *The Ottoman Empire*, 1300-1600, Phoenix

Ingamells, John, 1997: *Dictionary of British and Irish Travellers in Italy*, Yale

Jordan W.K., 1966: *The Chronicle and Political Papers of King Edward VI*, Allen and Unwin

Kelly, H.A., 1976: *The Matrimonial Trials of Henry VIII*, Stanford

Kennedy, Dane, 2005: *The Highly Civilized Man*, Harvard

Kenyon, John, 1972: *The Popish Plot*, Heinemann

Kenyon, J. and Ohlemeyer, J., 1990: *The Civil Wars*, Oxford

Knighton, C.S. (ed), 1992: *The State Papers of Edward VI*, HMSO, London

Leach, P., 1988: *James Paine*, A. Zwemmer

Loades, David, 1994: *The Reign of King Edward VI*, Headstart History

Loades, David, 2004: *Intrigue and Treason – the Tudor Court 1547-1558*, Longman

Lotherington, John, 2003: *The Tudor Years*, Hodder

Lovell, Mary S., 1998: *A Rage To Live*, Little, Brown & Company

Lucas, T., 1930: *Lives of the Gamesters*, Routledge

Lunn, David, 1998: *The Catholic Elizabethans*, Downside Abbey

McConnachie, J., 2007: *The Book of Love, In Search of the Kama Sutra*, Atlantic Books

Miller, J., 1973: *Popery and Politics in England 1660-1688*, Cambridge

Mingay, G.E., 1963: *English Landed Society in the 18th Century*, Routledge

Morey, A., 1978: *The Catholic Subjects of Elizabeth I*, Allen and Unwin

Nichols, J.G., 1848: *The Diary of Henry Machyn*, Camden Society, London

Nichols, J.G., 1852. *The Chronicle of the Grey Friars*, Camden Society, London

Northcote Parkinson, C., 1976: *Gunpowder Treason and Plot*, Weidenfeld

Oliver, S., 1857: *Collections Illustrating the History of the Catholic Religion*, London

The New Oxford Dictionary of National Biography, 2004, Oxford

Parker, R.A.C., 1975: *Coke of Norfolk*, Oxford

Parmiter, G., 1967: *The King's Great Matter*, Longmans

Parry, V., Inalcik N., 1976: *A History of Ottoman Imperialism*, Cambridge

Reid, L., 1969: *Charles James Fox: A Man For The People*, Longmans

Reid, P.R., 1952: *The Colditz Story*, Hodder

Reid, P.R., 1953: *The Latter Days at Colditz*, Hodder

Russell, J.G., 1969: *The Field of Cloth of Gold*, Routledge

Rutter, J., 1822: *An Historical and Descriptive Sketch of Wardour Castle*, Shaftesbury

Skidmore, C., 2007: *Edward VI: The Lost King of England*, Weidenfeld

Smiles, S., 2009: *Sir Joshua Reynolds*, Sansom, Bristol

Starkey, David, 2003: *Six Wives, The Queens of Henry VIII*, Chatto & Windus

Starkey, David, 1985: *The Reign of Henry VIII*, George Philip

Tucker, M., 1964: *The Life of Thomas Howard*, Mouton

Uglow, J., 2009: *A Gambling Man: Charles II and the Restoration*, Faber and Faber

Underdown, David, 1960: *Royalist Conspiracy in England, 1649-60*, Yale

Vickery, Amanda, 2009: *Behind Closed Doors*, Yale

Victoria History of the Counties of England, Wiltshire, vol 3

Webb, E., 1916: *Notes by the 12th Lord Arundell on the Arundell Family*, London

Weir, Alison, 2002: *Henry VIII, King and Court*, Pimlico

Williams, J.A., 1968: *Catholic Recusancy in Wiltshire 1606-1791*, Catholic Record Society

Williamson, B., 1982: *Wardour and the Arundells Not So Long Ago*, Bristol

Williamson, B., 1997: *Lord Arundell's Park at Wardour*, Bristol

Wordie, J.R., 1982: *Estate Management in 18th Century England*, Royal Historical Society

Wriothesley, Charles, 1875: *A Chronicle of England from 1485-1559*, Camden Society

Wroughton, John, 1999: *An Unhappy Civil War*, Lansdown

Young, Peter, 1974: *A Military History of the Three Civil Wars*, Methuen

Articles

Baumer, F.D., 1944: 'England, The Turk and the Common Corps of Christendom', *American Historical Review*, No 50

Beckett, J.V., 1977: 'English Landownership in the late 17th and 18th centuries – the debate and the problems', *Economic History Review*, second series, vol xxx

Cannadine, D., 1977: 'Landowners as Millionaires', *Agricultural History Review*, vol 25

Cowell, F., 1986-87: 'Richard Woods, a preliminary account', *Garden History*, vols 14 &15

Girouard, M., 1991: 'Wardour Old Castle', *Country Life*, vol 185, No 7

Habakkuk, J., 1950: 'Marriage Settlements in the 18th Century', *Transactions of the Royal Historical Society*, Fourth series, vol XXXII

Habbakkuk, J., 1979: 'The Rise and Fall of English Landed Families, 1600-1800', *Transactions of the Royal Historical Society*, Fifth series, vol XXXIX

Houlbrooke, R.A., 1994: 'Henry VIII's Wills: A Comment', *The Historical Journal*, 37

Ives, E.W., 1992: 'Henry VIII's Will: A Forensic Conundrum', *The Historical Journal*, 35

Krugler, John: 'The Face of a Protestant and the Heart of a Papist', *Church and State*

Krugler, John 1979: 'Lord Baltimore, Roman Catholics and Toleration', *Catholic Historical Review* 65

Krugler, John, 2004: 'The Calvert Vision: A New Model For Church-State Relations', *Maryland Historical Magazine*

Lunn, Maurus, 1971: 'Chaplains in the English Regiment in Spanish Flanders, 1605-1606', *Recusant History*, vol 11, No 3

Miller, Helen, 1978: 'Henry VIII's Unwritten Will,' *Wealth and Power in Tudor England* edited by E.W. Ives

Pears, Edwin, 1893: 'The Spanish Armada and the Ottoman Porte'. *English Historical Review*, vol VIII

Rawlinson, H.G., 1923: 'The Embassy of William Harborne in Constantinople', *Transactions of the Royal Historical Society*, Fourth series, V.

Rodwell, K.A., 1991: 'The Architecture of Entertainment', *Archaeological Journal*, vol 148

Root J. and Bryant J., 1994: 'The Kitchen Garden Buildings at New Wardour Castle', *English Heritage*

Spring, D., 1980: 'Aristocratic Indebtedness in the 19th Century', *Economic History Review*, second series vol XXXIII

Thompson, F.M.L., 1958: 'English Landownership: The Ailesbury Trust 1832-1856', *Economic History Review*, second series vol VIII

Wernham, R.B. 1987: 'Queen Elizabeth I, the Emperor Rudolph II and Archduke Ernest, 1593-94', *Politics and Society* by E. Kouri and T. Scott

Thank You

I F anyone has grown weary of the world and cynical of human nature, there is a simple remedy. Write a book involving prolonged research. You will have contact with dozens of kind people and you will be amazed at how helpful they are and generous with their time. Thank you to all the following:

The Hon. Richard Arundell, Melissa Atkinson of the National Portrait Gallery, the Rev. Cannon Thomas Atthill of Tisbury, Anton Bantock, Michael Barcroft, Ellie Barwise, Professor John Cannon, Morgan Cowles of English Heritage, Dr. Jane Cunningham of the Courtauld Institute, Ben Daubeny, Tim Dougall, Elizabeth Ellis, Bert Fairchild, Ivy Fackayan, Rose Gaynor, Professor John Guy, Christine Hughes, Assistant Archivist of the Sisters of Nazareth, Luke Hughes, Gill and Alastair Humphrey, Dave Johnson, Tony Keating, Mary Lovell, Stan Macey, Richard Maidment, Lisa Mannas, Henry Miller, Bernard Morgan, Jenny Morland, Professor Michael Mullett, Edmund Neville-Rolfe, Brian Osborne, Oliver Padel, Doreen Pastor, Callie Rodger, St. Deiniol's Library staff, John Savage, Rex Sawyer, Christine Shirley, Alison Spence of Cornwall Record Office, Dr. David Starkey, Liz Thorne, Jennifer Thorp, Archivist of New College, Oxford, Nigel Tuersley, the University of Bristol Library staff, Michael Whitfield, Gill and Hugh Woodeson and John Wroughton. I am sorry if I have forgotten anyone.

John Chandler has been a patient and supportive publisher. I am very lucky. So are all the Wiltshire people who have benefited from his publishing enterprises over the years. James Heritage of Clifton Colour worked tirelessly to scan the illustrations into high-resolution digital format. I can only admire his skill and thank him.

Lord Talbot of Malahide kindly gave me permission to see the family's accounts at Hoare's Bank and has been very helpful. Dr. Simon Johnson of Downside Abbey and David Knight, Archivist of Stonyhurst College have patiently answered more questions than it was right to ask them. Frank Hopton, the best of History teachers, has given me steadfast support and encouragement over the years. I am very grateful to them all.

Three people made me keen to start the research. Isabel Fagan, the last Lord Arundell's sister, asked me to write the story of the family in 1982 and talked with me about her childhood at Wardour. I found her love for Wardour and its people very moving. Martina Hoskins, Lady Arundell's parlour maid, shared her memories with me and let me enter a world that is as different from now as chalk from cheese. Les Parsons, the old thatcher in Ansty, most kind and gentle of men, told me his stories of a lifetime spent on the Wardour estate. I am sorry that a busy teaching life has made progress with this book so slow.

Steve Hobbs, at The Wiltshire and Swindon History Centre, has made the Centre a paradise for anyone working on Wiltshire families. If his archives were housed in tents on Salisbury Plain, his friendliness and encouragement would be the same. I am glad that his new, palatial building has not altered his style. All the History Centre staff have been very helpful and in particular I would like to thank Ian Hicks who has carried tons of Arundell papers from the storeroom to seat No 25.

Ann and Philip Revill invited me to stay with them in Hampton Court Palace in 2008 and the experience of walking at night through the half-lit rooms where Thomas Arundell once served Cardinal Wolsey and then King Henry VIII, made me keen to begin research. Gillian and Jeremy Hooper have been patient and ever helpful friends at Wardour, always prepared to answer 'one more question'.

Most important has been the tremendous encouragement and enthusiasm of the last Lord Arundell's nephew, Major General Patrick

Fagan. His kindness and patience in answering questions have been extraordinary and he arranged for the maps to be drawn by an expert. Without him, this book would not exist. I trust he is not too disappointed with the result. Obviously, the opinions and judgments are all mine, not his.

Lastly, my family. Writing a book puts a great strain on the whole family but as always they have been kind and very tolerant of living with the Arundells for the last two years. Sylvia has provided the perfect combination of encouragement, scepticism and practical help with photographs; Andy has been a brilliant proof-reader; Rachel and Sophie have been extremely supportive. I can only thank them for their generosity and love.

Barry Williamson
Bristol, Summer 2010

Pictures

I am grateful to the following for permission to use their pictures which appear on the pages indicated:

The Hon. Richard Arundell 60
The Ashmolean Museum, University of Oxford 130
Anton Bantock 71, 77
Christie's Images Ltd. 68, 93, 97, 107
Cornwall Record Office 5, 10
Country Life Picture Library 57, 132, 136, 137

The Courtauld Institute of Art, Photographic Survey 18, 19, 105

English Heritage 72

Major General Patrick Fagan 178, 179

Jeremy and Gillian Hooper 173, 175

The Imperial War Museum 195

The International Red Cross Archives, Geneva 198

Tony Keating 48

The National Archives 17

The National Portrait Gallery, London 108, 153

His Grace the Duke of Norfolk 18, 19

Brian Osborne 192

Sothebys 99

Stonyhurst College 144

Lord Talbot of Malahide 38

Tate Britain 92

Tisbury Local History Society 39

The Trustees of Wardour Chapel 14

Nigel Tuersley 124, 135, 138

The Weiss Gallery 82

The Williamson Archive   27, 28, 33, 45, 46, 47, 56, 64, 69, 73, 85, 91,
        122, 128, 131, 155, 165, 196, 200

The Wiltshire and Swindon History Centre viii, 3, 22, 24, 31, 40, 55, 58,
        59, 79, 90, 94, 106, 125, 126, 128, 129, 138, 140, 142, 143,
        160, 163, 169, 172, 186

Gill Woodeson 167

All the maps, except that of Cornwall, have been drawn by David Johnson.

Index

This index includes people, places and selected subjects. The notes have not been indexed.